AWAKENING
THE
EVOLUTIONARY
SPIRIT

To Martha + Elizabeth.

Nov 10, 2007

The Evolutionary Spirit will speak to your heart and you will know the Joy of Love !

Margaret Barry

AWAKENING THE EVOLUTIONARY SPIRIT

Revelations of an Anawim

Margaret Barry

Library of Congress Control Number: 2004195385
ISBN: Hardcover   978-1-4134-8111-2
                     Softcover   978-1-4134-8110-5

This book was printed in the United States of America.

To order additional copies of this book, contact:
Xlibris Corporation
1-888-795-4274
www.Xlibris.com
Orders@Xlibris.com
27213

CONTENTS

Reflections

Titles of Poems

With love and gratitude, I dedicate this book to the wonderful women in my life, my mother Connie, my aunt Esther, and the teaching Sisters of St. Joseph.

For those who have eyes to see let them see.

About the Author,
About the Book

The inspirations captured within these pages are a result of the personal experience of an awakening that came from deep within my self. It brought about an awareness of Being, an awareness in which I began a journey in discovering who I am and who God is. At first I did not realize how important this experience was, but over a period of time, recognition of its importance became manifest. This story, told in poetry and reflections, is not for me alone but for all searching souls who wish to know what is at the core and source of their existence.

While my background is that of a Catholic Christian, the insights expressed herein have come from the Holy Spirit, for no human being has taught me what I have come to know through my experiences in awareness and enlightenment.

Sometimes when I speak of Christ, I am not just speaking about Jesus the Christ. Christ is "the anointed one" who has been and is in all major religions of the world, though perhaps called by a different name. Christ is of the Spirit, neither male nor female. Christ is in the one whose eyes have been opened, the enlightened one who follows the narrow path. The Christ of which I speak is cosmic and incorporated into all flesh. It is a beneficial duty for every cell of flesh in the world to discover Christ—their self within who is waiting to awaken and enlighten every human being.

Growing up in a New England mill town during the 1940s and 50s, with multiethnic immigrants, including my grandparents, was one of the most enriching experiences of my early life. I was richly rewarded for being an observer of life around me. I saw people who worked hard, loved with quiet, unspoken intensity and did all within their power to make life good and share their wholesome standards. Then there were a few self absorbed who seemed unable to commit either to work or to love. Their passion was in being angry at the world. Upon noticing these differences, there was within me a growing conscious decision to work well, do good and try my best to love, with the hope to be loved. Thus began my spiritual journey in life, while I was not yet aware of where this decision would take me, the price I would pay, or the joys I would know for the choice I had made.

My story began about the age of six years when outstanding thoughts began to come to my mind, thoughts that were imprinted like a laser beam cut into a recording. There would be the call to priesthood, the prediction of my mother's death, a child's struggle to survive amid poverty and unsavory characters. There was the disbelief and rejection by priests of my religion. There was enlightenment with my experience, which gave me the perseverance to continue. I knew this knowledge was given to me from a higher power and no matter how I was treated for my beliefs, I would not give up what I had been told and knew in my soul that things would come to pass in God's good time and in God's way.

It was February 23, 1965, when I actually made the statement that I had become *aware of Being*. Initially I had attributed this statement to God and began writing down my thoughts. Upon reflecting what was written, I saw that I was writing about myself. While my concentration was fixed upon God—the other outside of me—it came about that what was being revealed was the self within. God is both within and outside of all creatures.

New insights and revelations were constant through nature and through the physical and spiritual world that surrounded me. My mind was deluged with experiential knowledge, which came predominantly by way of observation and reflection, through reason. It is an enlightenment that has changed my life forever. This is what I have written about. Writing became a necessity in my life for it was difficult to find someone with whom intimate thoughts could be shared. *I have come to realize that intimacy with another person is only possible when it is reciprocal.* Still, I knew that these special thoughts were not for me alone. They were the thoughts of a mystic and are to be given to the people of God's creation. The writings began to take on a vision that became a big picture, like a giant puzzle, pieces were fitting together. They told a story. The spiritual connected to the physical, the psychological and the scientific. Ultimately everything connected to the cosmos and to God.

This is expressed in a subtle but unmistakable manner. It is expressed in the simplest terms throughout these writings. They tell a story of an evolving spirit that is at once both personal and cosmic.

The road I have traveled these past forty years has been with pain and joy. While I know the hand of God has been guiding me all of my life, I am now more eager than ever to tell all the people of God of the possibilities that lie in store for his beloved creations. When I was troubled and afraid, which was many times, there was only the Lord for me to turn to. He told me to do this, *"Ask and you will receive, seek and you will find, knock and the door will be opened to you" (Luke 11:9)*. These are trustworthy words. They gave birth to this mystic, *a new* woman. It has given me cause to believe that a new world of people is about to emerge with a new consciousness, a new spirit of awareness, becoming the epitome of our creator's design, the Omega person.

At this time I have come to believe that the experiences expressed in my reflections and poems are a parallel experience of the feminine of God, which is the Holy Spirit of God, who has been attempting to be in union and at oneness with human beings. She has been overlooked, ignored, rejected and even denied, by blind, male dominated, feudal, hierarchical religions. But the evolution of *our* species which is becoming more and more like its creator is entering a phase of experiencing the awakening or awareness of Being, which will unite us not only to God but to one another in order that a Cosmic Christ will be born.

I

The Child and the Call

My story about *the call* has to do with nuptials, weddings, or what otherwise might be called unions with God; and the sacraments experienced here, are internalized, deeply personal and spiritual, not ritualized. It is also a sensual story and at the same time sacred. It is an invitation from the Spirit and from nature to accept the revelation of one's *self* when we recognize that God is within all and will speak to us in our consciousness if we pay attention.

It began with an innocent and naive child of about six years, in her first year of school. She really loved to listen to people talk. It made her feel like she was part of everybody around her—as if she belonged. Everything seemed so interesting. One of the things she enjoyed hearing about most was the greatness and goodness of God . . . how big he was and the wonderful things he could do.

Sister Carmel told the children that this wonderful person, who made the whole world, everybody, and everything in it, cared about each one of us, that he loved us and wanted to talk to us, and that he wanted us to talk to him. Sister said God would make us wise and intelligent if we listened to him. And a little girl at the age of six, who did not feel at all smart, made a wish in her heart that God would talk to her and make her intelligent. And there was a sweet voice within her that spoke and said, "*When you're older, God will talk with you.*" "Older" seemed like a long way off. She wanted to be intelligent **now.** She wanted God to talk to her now. There was just silence. But she did believe and trusted in what she heard. She would wait in hope to be intelligent.

One day at Sunday Mass, as she was kneeling in the front row of church and her eyes were just able to see over the kneeling board in front of her, she looked up at the mural on the church ceiling . . . and there was God, with his long white beard and stern look. The child needed to talk to him. But she couldn't look at him. So she lowered her head and closed her eyes. And in the quiet of her heart she said, "God, my daddy is not good to my mommy. I don't want a husband like him. Please send me a good husband when I grow up." She repeated that little prayer many times during her young life.

And when she was older she wrote,

The Wedding

> I went up to the house of my Lord,
> and upon His altar burned
>   twelve innocent lights.
>
> And there were placed two personal
> bouquets of red within white.
> Thought came to know
>   a new bride and groom.
>
> Upon seeing—, my heart caught fire
> and burned as the light of the sun.
> His Spirit flowed to my lips
>   and salt was tasted upon my tongue.
>
> Intensely in my body did I feel
> Him tremble through me.
>   Now we're nourished by our Being
>   in this ever burning flame of Love.
>
> 1967

Was this the answer to a child's prayer?

Life moved on, and it was about three years later that this little girl left school one day, apparently in a happy mood, for she was skipping across the school yard over toward the church. Then all of a sudden she stopped; she heard a rather imperative voice that said, "You will be my priest." She stood motionless for a moment, somewhat in wonder, but then continued to bounce down the walkway. The impression left by those words would be stored her mind, where from time to time they would resurface.

It was a few years later, perhaps at the age of eleven that another memorable event occurred. (Strange how some experiences remain etched upon the brain.) One day while playing in the schoolyard, the priest who was the assistant pastor called the young girl over to talk with him. He asked about the game the kids were playing, and then he came around to ask if she was going to be a nun when she grew up. She said, "no," in a hesitating manner. But he pursued further and then asked, "What are you going to be when you grow up?" Without hesitation, the young girl replied, "I want to be a priest." For a moment he stood speechless but replied with a smile "Well, it looks like the next big revelation for the church will come from outside the church." (I guess lay people were considered to be *outside* the church in those days (about 1948) and only the clergy were *in*.) It was then that she began to realize that she had never seen a woman priest and wondered if there were any. Anyhow, he and the nuns were always kind and patient with the young dreamer and slow learner. Visits to church were important to her, as she did not want Jesus to be alone, as sister suggested he was.

Then when she was older she wrote,

The Call

"You will be My Priest."
Be calm my soul, for the Lord
my God has *anointed* you
with the oil of gladness.

Rejoice, you who bear the mark of
my son upon your brow,
your breast and tongue.

Be calm my soul and come
　　with me
to the wedding celebration.
This gift and garment
　　befits this wonderful occasion—
The banquet of the King.

Be calm my soul,
　　sit by my side.
Drink from my cup.
　　Taste the fruit of my vine.
The bread of my labor is
　　food for your life.

Be calm my soul, for the Lord
　　my God has *anointed* you
with the oil of gladness.
　　Be glad!　　Rejoice!
Celebrate the festival—
　　this Wedding of Love to Life.

1968

The *call* is to the priesthood of Christ, as Peter tells us, *But you are "a chosen race, a royal priesthood, a holy nation, a people of his own, so that you may announce the praises"* of him who called you out of darkness into his wonderful light. (One Peter 2:9). Peter is speaking about people who have not just received a water baptism but those who have also received the baptism of the Holy Spirit, into his "wonderful light." And in *(Heb 5:6)* we read, *"You are a priest forever according to the order of Melchizedek."* In this priesthood we are called to another nuptial, being *one* with the Father, as Jesus is *one* with the Father. The order of Melchizedek is that order of Christ, the eternally begotten one.

Now this young lady kept in very close contact with God through the years, especially in her aloneness and when there were problems.

When she was thirteen years old, her mother was killed by a drunk driver who ran over her with his lumber truck. There had been a warning about it the evening before when she said good night to her mother, . . . that voice again. "That's the last time you will see your mother alive." And so it was.

The aloneness was terrible. Her dad drank too much and his friends from the bar were scary to have around. But there was a refuge, and the young girl ran for comfort. I'll tell you about the prayer that was in her heart, because *when she was older*, she wrote . . .

Weeping Light

She was just a child with
    a heavy heart and pitiful thoughts.

I saw through eyes that cried while
    she knelt before
        the image and prayed
            to the person it reminded her of,
and I heard her say;

"I am so lonesome, so afraid.
What's to become of me?
I ask your guidance.
Be my mother, please."

And she wept thought upon thought,
    'til her being was relieved, and
        she was content.

I saw through eyes the tears
    the image cried for her—
        a streak of light,
            an answered prayer;
She knew!

What a consolation to know that Mary cared. She was the one who guided the child through those tender years. But now high school years were ending. The girl needed to be free from helplessness, for all she had been able to do was passively accept what life was handing her. She knew things had to change. The shell of childhood was abruptly broken and by necessity, I began to emerge. There was a great need within me to be far removed from a very impoverished environment.

I had been offered a small scholarship to college and I thought it would be a chance to improve my life, be of service to people and to God. However, my relatives sputtered and fumed at me, "Who do you think you are that you should go to college?" I forgot about college and accepted the marriage proposal of a sailor. Perhaps this marriage would be the answer to a child's prayer. (How little we know at eighteen.) Thoughts about the priesthood were forgotten (for a while). The soul needed to evolve and that would take many years. It would only happen as a result of life's learning experiences, with its pain and joy, good and bad, tragedy and triumph, the fullness of what is human and the intervention of the divine.

Something was missing from the marriage. There was uncertainty in my heart. Had I done the right thing in marrying someone who knew so very little about Christianity? Should there be more to marriage than I was experiencing? All at once I made the decision to *make the best of it,* come what may. Acceptance of the decision brought contentment within. It was several months after that when the nesting desire had set in. But there was only disappointment and pain because of the many miscarriages. Doctors said it was unlikely that there would ever be any children. Belief in the power of prayer and faith in God's goodness would bring results! Mary would listen and tell Jesus about this matter. Besides, I promised to name my first baby girl Mary.

She was perfect and beautiful—another answered prayer. A couple of years went by, and as I watched and enjoyed the gift of this child, there was a very strong desire within me to "do it again"—have another child. But my husband was still in college with another year to go, and he had no desire for another child. Yet, a seed had been planted in his mind and love does win out. As a result there was an awesome experience of two human souls bonded in a spiritually sexual union in oneness with God.

Later I wrote about this special experience.

Awaken Love

"Wake my Love, Awake!
The voice of God just spoke to me."

He bound from a bed of slumber
　　with excitement in his being,
searching desperately through darkness
　　to see the voice which he was hearing.

"What are you saying, featherhead?
Be still and come to bed."

"Listen, listen, yes its true!
I heard Him!
Listen, perhaps you'll hear Him too."

"I hear nothing.
What about you?"

"He told me to go to you, and if you love . . .
A son I'll have, and he will be great.
The word is truth I state!"

"Never mind, it matters not.
Come, I can but give."

And giving gave for love of life.
　　And loving was exceptionally,
wonderfully new!
　　Rapture, wonder, bliss beyond telling.
Exhilarating! Electrifying!
　　The Spirit of God in ecstasy, inundating!
Penetrating depths and bounties
　　Once unknown to the soul.

After loving came much thought.
This indeed is true.

Then seeing through a starlit night
thought knew . . .
God's in his heaven,
all's well in his world!

1967

I believe God wants all his people *to know* the beauty, sacredness and pleasure of sexual love and that God truly is *present and active* in this union. The calling of God to a man and woman into this spiritual experience of sexual love is none other than the revelation of the nature of *God in humanity* and a reflection of the eternal reality. Our creator has designed holy pleasure into the lovemaking of his creatures. I believe that this kind of knowledge about sexual relationships needs to be taught by the church to the people of God. In actuality, a vast number of Christians already know *by experience* that they have encountered the spiritual, the mystical, the holy one in their act of love for one another. Yet some have had this experience and cannot name it! How is it that teachers of God have not (because they cannot?) informed God's people of such matters? Our church must learn to know and teach more of this vital truth to God's people and shout it from the rooftops. It must honor the beauty of sexuality, sexual love, and God's revelation of his nature in and with man and woman.

So there was David, then Barry and Deborah and Timothy and Daniel. David died in a car accident just after his twentieth birthday. Baby Daniel lived but two days, and I almost died when he was born.

In between children, I used to wonder if I could only please God by pleasing the church regarding their laws prohibiting birth control. What is meant by natural? *Is everything that is natural right and good?* Are the many *different* conditions in my life and in the lives of all *different* people taken into consideration by church law? There were many questions and many prayers. There were weeks of prayers, seeking answers. Then the time came when I said, "Jesus, *you* have got to tell me!" Finally there was the prayer that became emphatic and heartfelt. "I want *you* to tell me what to do. I am only a human being with human limitations. *You said* you would help if I asked! I remember your words . . . *"I tell you, ask and you will receive; seek and you will find; knock and the door will be opened to you."* *(Luke 11:9) You* gave your word; I want *you* to keep your word!" Days and weeks of repeated begging, pleading, bartering and asking an answer from God went by. But through all the seeking and frustration there emerged some *new thinking,* which had little to do with my demands about an answer to the birth-control problem.

Lovely, new, beautiful, awesome, inspiring thoughts were filling my mind. Was the world changing? The change was the world within. *Light* was being let in. New life was being revealed. Eyes were being opened. All things were becoming new . . . amazing and wonderful. Familiar words came to mind, *"I am the light of the world."* *(Jn 9:5)* And this lady began to wonder if God himself might be seeing his creation through her eyes and delighting in all that was being taken in through her senses. (That was February 23, 1965).

Why this new thinking? Why was I overcome by it all? Why was God so intense in my mind? What does it mean?

I went to see Fr. Philip (a Vincentian priest, in Panama at that time). As I spoke, relating the events of my new thinking, he began to cry. Thinking that I had said something out of place, I asked, "Why are you crying?" "You have seen God," he said. Shaking my head in disbelief, I said, "I have seen his love." "God is love," he said. For the first time in my life, at the age or twenty-seven, I had heard "God is love"! Why hadn't anyone told me this before? After a while, I bought a Bible from him. I began to read it. (Something I had previously been forbidden to do by the church.) The Holy Spirit began to give new life to ancient words! In church, the scriptures were beginning to be read in English! They suddenly became *living, meaningful* words.

Immediately, the floodgates of heaven were opened! God is love! But LOVE is everywhere! The honeymoon began. I began to KNOW God! And in knowing God, his greatness, his goodness, his love and beauty, one becomes humbled, even humiliated by one's sinfulness, and the recognition of one's littleness. There is immediate contrition at this awareness. Then, with contrition came a blessing!

The Coming of Love

O, Lord, I am not worthy,
  was my prayer to you that day.
I was remembering my blessings
  when you took my breath away.

I must confess . . .

"O my God, I am heartily sorry
  for having offended thee,
because you are all good,
  and deserving of all my love . . ."

Then a stirring deep inside me,
  dread of hell could not abide.

This *presence* overwhelms me.
  He's miraculously inside.
I cannot speak, I cannot think.
  There's just this knowing . . .
He's in my being!

Oh, how I'm blest to know his favor.
  He's for me and I'm for him!
Lord, I'll always know and recognize
  Your movement in my soul.
My thoughts of thanks are never enough.
  You've made my being whole.

Yes, it was many weeks ago
  my being filled and overflowed of you,
To bestow a lovely mystery.

  "You are all good
and deserving of all my love."
  Stay with me, evermore.

"O my God . . ."

1965

I was sweeping the floor in the living room when the Spirit of God came upon me. There I stood motionless, as wave upon wave of that overwhelming presence moved upon me, from the top of my head down though my entire body and into my feet. I cannot say how long it lasted, at least several minutes. The experience left me speechless and joyful. It left me with a sense of euphoria for that entire day and many days thereafter.

What is experienced here is what Jesus spoke to Nicodemus about, *"Amen, amen, I say to you, no one can see the kingdom of God without being born from above." "No one can enter the kingdom of God without being born of water and Spirit." (Jn 3:3,5)* Then, John the Baptist says of Jesus: *"He will baptize you with the Holy Spirit and fire" (Mt 3:11),* i.e., the fire of love.

"The Spirit and the bride say, "Come." Let the hearer say, "Come." Let the one who thirsts come forward, and the one who wants it receive the gift of life-giving water." (Rev 22:17) People need to *ask* Jesus to come into their lives. He will. That's all anyone needs to do is *ask*. Then the Spirit of Christ will take us to himself and enrapture us, his bride, with a powerful and mighty love. This is an experience of being in union with God. It is being one in relationship with the consciousness of God and creation.

So at the age of twenty-seven, *at last I was older.* God was talking to me. I was listening. And I was talking to him. A child's prayerful wish had come to be. I was intelligent! The *living water* flowed. Jesus said to the woman at the well, *"but whoever drinks the water I shall give will never thirst; the water I shall give will become in him a spring of water welling up to eternal life." (Jn 4:14)* Gifts of the Holy Spirit became continuous and intense . . . There were inspirations, insights, personal and cosmic revelations, prayers, prophecy, wisdom, teachings, and writings. There was strength, patience, pain, joy, suffering, and growth in truth. But as Paul tells us in 1 Corinthians 13, the greatest gift is LOVE . . . Because love is the gift of God himself, living and active within us.

Is it any wonder that Jesus *commanded* us to love? *"I give you a new commandment: love one another. As I have loved you, so you also should love one another." (Jn 13:34)* He wanted us to exercise this most powerful of energy—love, to exercise the Spirit of God, our creator within, and spend this energy building a better life for a new and better world.

Awareness of the beauty of this loving union with God still overwhelms me. Excitement still surges through my being when I am engaged in spiritual intercourse with him. There is openness and oneness in our relationship. Jesus knew this experience well: *"I am in the Father and the Father is in me . . ." (Jn 14:11)*

Unity

Now, this very day, my Being is full.
My work is not in vain.
I stretch forth my hand—reach out to you
through my son; to touch
your hand, your heart, your mind.
His labors have won me a prize . . .
A living body, a loving people, a beautiful family,
Looking up . . . reaching out . . .
with praise to me.

I will comfort you in every way, and be your joy
throughout all the days of your life.
Forever my hand is extended . . .
and you have grown now from childhood
into a people of understanding.
I live in him, and he lives in you.
And he in you, reaching out to me,
responds with dearest love.

I speak to you of my word,
and give to you with love,
the image of my Being,
in every man and woman.
I call to you and you respond
through my spirit in your life.
I reach down to you in love.
You reach up to me with prayer and praise.
I live in you.
And your life is within me.
We are becoming one another!

Father, you answer my prayer today,
forevermore, and always.
You live in me, and I in you; and further,
my brothers and sisters have accepted us.
We live in them, for see,
they're reaching out with our love
to touch each other.
They're touching you and me!

So in my spirit I give
to unite us all as One.
I pour out my Spirit to fill your flesh
and flow from one to another.
I move in the name of Christ, my incarnate word.
His flesh covers all my people.

This kind of unity is the trinity of God evolving in individuals and in our world. This evolving spirit is the coming of Christ into our lives, individually and collectively.

"I am the light of the world." (Jn 8:12) He is the light that gives enlightenment. And that enlightenment is about the knowledge of God and the love of God. *It becomes us*, it becomes our life, our source and our fulfillment. This light brings enlightenment to the anointed ones in every religion of God's creation.

"I will ask the Father, and He will give you another Advocate to be with you always," and again, *"I will not leave you orphans; I will come back to you" (Jn14:16,18).* Jesus keeps his promise; he will, and he does come back to us again and again. His spirit is with us in all the actions and activities of our lives. He is living and loving through us. He is creating *His kingdom* through us.

Having Jesus in my life is the greatest blessing and experience of my life. It has not always been easy. My husband was not a baptized person, and he did not understand my experiences. He was even fearful when I spoke about God. He told a clergyman about it, who advised him to *"put her away."* So I was taken against my will to a mental institution. After three days, (It was the fourth of July weekend.) I met with the psychiatrist who told me I was free to go home. But in my anger at my husband, I requested to stay, and the doctor allowed me to do so. After a few weeks there, I wanted to return to my children, which I did. Now I can thank God for laws that were passed during the women's liberation movement. The law no longer permits a husband to *put his wife away* for just any reason, not even for speaking about the coming of the Spirit of Christ into her life.

After seventeen years of marriage there was a divorce. This was a difficult time, worrying about how I would manage with five children, the mortgage, the bills and all, but even and especially then, God did not leave me, and when I went to him in desperation, he revealed his love and mercy!

Ascent from Desperation

In desperation, O Lord, I called your name.
Jesus Christ, Jesus Christ, Jesus Christ,
over and over and over again.

And you reached down in gentleness
and with your breath
drew up my spirit from that shell of flesh,
which sat like a corpse on the seat below.

It mattered not.
My Lord had called.
I had to go . . .

His power drew me up and on to him
into the highest heaven,
where I lingered while he lavished
untold thoughts of Love
upon my spiritual being.

With no measure of time in the infinite,
It's hard to say how long I stayed.
Then he brought me back
to my body, renewed,
filled with the food of him—
the gracious gift of his mercy.

Later as I walked along, all but
a faint reminder of that inexpressible
mystical experience was gone,
and all I could say was,
"God, that was nice!
Thank you.
O God, how I thank you!"

1971

(See Two Corinthians 12:1-4)

So, for about twenty years and more, the Spirit was continuously teaching me, but I was not always able to tell anyone about it. It was taboo to speak about God, especially for a woman, and I was forced to write. The old pastor in my parish told me to go home, do my dishes, take good care of my children, and not to think about these things. Looking for a spiritual director from 1965 onward (as I was advised to do by the priest in Panama) only led to disappointment after disappointment, and I began to wonder if some priests had ever received the Holy Spirit. Their detachment seemed unchristian and dehumanizing.

When charismatic prayer meetings came along, it was a joy for me to be able to share my thoughts of God. When prayer meetings faded away, or were discouraged by the church, I began to turn off the Spirit (truly God is too much to bear without telling), and I became engrossed in my work as a printer. For more than a dozen years, I had little or no time for church or clergy. I was not accepted, not able to be involved. The clergy, or the church, was not involved with me. It seemed like the message of the church was, lay people must not speak about the Good News; that would be reserved for clergy alone.

About five years ago, (1997) a priest came to our parish who invited people to participate and volunteer in parish activities. Did I dare? . . . Yes, eventually, and it was nice: Bible study, teaching the kids catechism, retreats, trips, potluck supper, etc. Then the Spirit was revived again for me when a gifted spiritual woman came to our parish, shared her music and the love of the Lord. For the first time in about a dozen years, I went to confession. It felt good to start my journey back . . . experience a beginning to some very necessary healing. Eventually I became a lay minister. I am enjoying the Spirit of the Lord in my life again as he intends, and as I love; not that he ever left me. It was I who was unfaithful to him.

When I think about the adversities I have experienced along life's path, I am filled with strength and confidence especially when I read the Lord's message to me in Isaiah 62. And this message is for all of us. We, God's people are His New Jerusalem, his bride, his love, his body, and his church.

Several years ago, about 1995, I began to realize that I would never be ordained a Roman Catholic priest, but then I also realized that Jesus was never ordained a Roman Catholic priest either. He was *anointed the Christ, begotten from above.* While the institutional church has not allowed women to be ordained priests, the Holy Spirit calls and anoints whomever s/he will. Anointing to Christ's priesthood comes from above. I am content with this priesthood.

These days, when I attend Mass, it is at the offertory, the elevation of the bread and wine—these elements of life-giving spirit and energy—that I offer my life experiences to God, with and *as His priest.* Therein does the spiritual transformation take place, and I, along with all the people of God, can say in Christ, "This is my body! This is my blood!" These words are also recalled when I share meals with friends and relatives in our homes.

In the third chapter of Galatians, verse twenty-eight, Paul tells us that for we who are clothed in Christ, by our baptism, *"There is neither Jew nor Greek, there is neither slave nor free person, there is not male and female; for you are all one in Christ Jesus."* We are one in Christ, and as Christ.

1999
Revised 2005

II

Life, Labor, and the Holy Eucharist

Because of the many parables that Jesus told about vineyards, wheat fields, shepherds and fishermen, one cannot help but think that these were the places he worked, learned, and participated in life, with people and with the earth, (*like His Father/Creator*). This is where he grew in wisdom, observing and *experiencing* human nature and elevating it to the spiritual. When Jesus spoke in parables, truly he was speaking out of his own personal experiences. While he was the "carpenter's son," it is very likely he worked as a carpenter. But was there always work for a carpenter to do? If not, what else might he have done to earn his livelihood?

Imagine Jesus when he was out in a boat with Peter and the other fishermen. Peter and his crew had fished all night long and had caught nothing, but Jesus said, *"Put out into the deep water and lower your nets for a catch." (Luke 5:4)* They did so and got the catch that Jesus expected they would. Do you think that Jesus just stood and watched? Can you imagine him pulling on the net with the fishermen helping them haul in the catch that almost broke their net? *Jesus knew what it was to labor.* He also turned his fishermen into "fishers of men." In the Gospels, he speaks of labor and laborers many times and in many ways.

We know about the public life of Jesus as recorded in the Gospels. We have to assume things about his life prior to that time. We have to assume that he did work for a living and that *what he experienced as a laborer was many times related in his parables.* He taught us about heavenly or spiritual things through human and natural events.

In Matthew, chapter twenty there is the story of men who had been working all day in a vineyard: they were standing in line for their pay; there were some who received a full day's pay when they only worked part of a day. There were complaints from those who did a whole day's work and were not paid more. Do you think Jesus experienced this event, perhaps while standing in line? Truly he worked, observed, and then taught the positive side of that situation. He saw the owner of the vineyard as a generous man. Jesus related these human events to the divine, revealing God our Father's goodness in rewarding us for our *labors,* no matter how long or short we labor.

Jesus and his disciples were walking through a wheat field on the Sabbath. They picked the grains of wheat to eat, as they were hungry. This was considered *work* by the Pharisees who condemned them, but Jesus defended their right to eat and work, even on the Sabbath (Mt 12:1-8).

Then we have the experience of Jesus watching, perhaps even helping some woman, most likely his mother Mary, when he was a child; it is then that one is taken with curiosity and amazement at watching the making of bread and the working of yeast and the rising of the dough. Such impressions can last a lifetime . . . and then a wonderful analogy for the reign of God develops! It is a *working,* growing, developing experience in which he lived and we are called to participate in (Lk 13:20-21).

The power of God bathes the world with *energy.* There is magnetism in the light of the Creator, which draws the broken seed out of the earth to produce new life. From roots in the earth grow the vine and the branches—*"I am the vine, you are the branches." (Jn 15:5)* The vine and the branches together produce the fruit of the vine—wine—, which we drink as his life's blood. We drink *our* life's blood—the *energy* and work of *God in His people.* That same light and magnetism draws on the spirit in every human being to grow and flourish in the Spirit of Christ. We *are* a *work* in progress. While we are experiencing this work, this *energy* that is being spent, we are *experiencing* the Spirit of God within and around us.

"Blessed are you, Lord, God of all creation. Through your goodness we have this wine to offer, fruit of the vine and *work of human hands.* It will become our spiritual drink."

By our *work,* spending *our energy,* whether it be as the farmer, who does the planting and harvesting, or the waitress, office or factory worker at the daily grind, teacher, parent, scientist, writer, artist—workers in all areas of life spending mental, spiritual, or physical energy, by free will, we know that this is the *Spirit* at work in the body—our individual bodies, as well as the **world body**. One can say that it is by the Spirit and, or, *energy* of God that we live, move, work and have our Being. It is the *Spirit of Christ* that is continuously at *work* in us.

All this spent *energy*—*this Spirit*—what more can be said of it or done with it? Those of us who believe in God offer it to Him, as a *sacrifice,* in thanks and praise, and when we do, it transforms and sanctifies us, hour-by-hour, day by day. Spiritual growth happens: we become greater in the person of Christ, and we are brought to a new level in our humanity and divinity.

"Amen, amen, I say to you, unless the grain of wheat falls to the ground and dies, it remains just a grain of wheat; but if it dies, it produces much fruit." (Jn 12:24) Again a "work" is in progress: the natural, the human, and the divine. The seed of heaven, Jesus Christ, was planted upon our earth. It is here that he lived, worked, and died and produced abundant fruit through his particular labors, which have lived and grown for more than two thousand years. We who love him continue to bear the fruit that his labor began. The Spirit of Christ, which we have inherited, gives us the energy to produce "much fruit" in all we do—our work, joys, or suffering—in our struggles with living, loving, evolving, developing, becoming . . . Christ in us again, continually.

The efforts from the *energy of the Spirit* in us, build and bind us together in the Body of Christ. *"Take and eat; this is my body."* (Mt 26:26) As Christ holds bread of life in his hands, he holds the *elements of the world,* for bread comes from the wheat and wheat comes from the seed and the seed comes out of the earth; and we the people of God's creation have come out of the earth too. Our body is his body. At the consecration of these elements, Christ is holding the whole world and all his people in his hands. In essence he is saying of all creation, with all of us together, "This is my body. This is my blood." Jesus the Christ has given us the example—spent his life's energy and died to reveal how the elements of the earth, all of us, are transformed by His Spirit.

We consume the energy that gives us life. "Blessed are you, Lord, God of all creation. Through you goodness we have this bread to offer, which earth has given and human hands have made. It will become for us the

32

bread of life." The **elements of nature**—the **elements of life**—are Spirit and become spiritualized in us! His presence lives in us, and we in him. We consume his life, his Spirit, and his energy. As we spend these gifts, we too are consumed and offer them to God in Christ. The efforts, energy, and labors of love are unending.

What is it besides work that captures our energy, our love, our spirit? Who among us has not experienced sorrow and joy? The Eucharist is the Pascal experience . . . a memorial, Jesus says, *"This is my body, which will be given for you; do this in memory of me". (Lk 22:19)* Christ has died. When we suffer, in any way—a death of family or friend, sickness, loss of income, and, to many in the world, hunger and oppression, lack of the necessities of life—there is a dying that is taking place in the human person, an energy that consumes . . . *This we offer to God as sacrifice.* "This is my body. This is my blood."

Now Christ is raised! He has overcome death and sin. That part of us that has died by our suffering is now risen with Christ, and we have experienced a transformation in his Spirit, grown strong, and live to experience this event over again until we reach the full stature of the Spirit of Christ. And what of our joy? Life's efforts produce its joys too. This is also offered to God. It is *the fruit of the vine* that we can savor, and no one can take it from us!

Human energy spent in works, sorrows, joys, and growth are spent willingly. We do the *duties* (labors) that life calls us to because it is none other than the power and Spirit of love that has possession of us.

There are those today who would deny the presence of Christ in the Eucharist. That is like denying life, love, spirit, and energy in the human person. But because we know the *Spirit* of Christ—that life-giving **force** of love—we know his presence in the world, within us, and within the Holy Eucharist. In our participation of this Eucharist, we are also participating in our own salvation and redemption story. Jesus has shown us *the way* in which we must live, labor, and love with His Spirit.

October 21, 1999

III

Begotten from Above,
The Christ Experience

There have been many important questions posed with regard to the priesthood of Christ. It would take inspirations from the Holy Spirit to arrive at acceptable answers. Yet, could it be that the Holy Spirit has given the answers, but the institutional church has stood in the way of our view as to what the Spirit has to tell us very clearly from scripture?

I am pleased and not at all surprised that we have so many women called to priesthood. Some have claimed priesthood through "ordination" which the teaching church does not recognize. However, I have to ask, how many who have been called to the priesthood have *claimed* the priesthood as revealed in the life of Jesus the Christ? Jesus was not ordained and the apostles were not ordained in the manner of ordination as we are familiar with today, but they did receive the anointing of the Holy Spirit and herein is the lovely mystery of the priesthood of Christ revealed.

Please let me explain:

"After Jesus was baptized, he came up from the water and behold, the heavens were opened [for him], and he saw the Spirit of God descending like a dove {and} coming upon him. * *And a voice came from the heavens, saying, "This is my beloved Son,* * *with whom I am well pleased." (Matthew 3:16-17).* A *spiritual birthing* had just taken place as "the heavens were opened," for the Holy Spirit of God had given birth to the Christ. Jesus was washed and baptized in the waters of the earth and then *spiritually begotten* by the Holy Spirit from above. For all who witnessed the baptism of Jesus, they saw an external event take place. But there is more. The Spirit of God had just anointed Jesus as the Christ. No one laid hands on Jesus and no one poured oil on him, but an awesome inward event took place within him. He now had the need to be alone

with the Spirit that had just entered him. He was driven into the desert for forty days and nights to fast and pray. The Holy Spirit would be instructing and teaching Jesus. *(Mark 1:13) says "... angels ministered to him",* and he was tempted in every way, yet resisted and overcame the evil one. The order of these events is important in that we are to follow the way and experience that Jesus lived out for us as an example. The water baptism represents repentance and the washing away of sin, our sins that Jesus took upon himself. We know that Jesus was without sin, and John believing this, was reluctant to baptize Jesus. But Jesus told him, *"Allow it now, for thus it is fitting for us to fulfill all righteousness." (Mt 3:15)* Our Father had a plan and in the life of Jesus, an example is being presented to us. Upon showing us that repentance is first in order, the Holy Spirit then enters in.

"Begotten" is a word we speak each time we say the Nicene Creed. **"We believe in one Lord, Jesus Christ, the only Son of God, eternally begotten of the Father, God from God, Light from Light, true God from true God, begotten, not made, one in Being with the Father."** In this portion of the creed, our focus is on a spiritual birth, for Christ is not made but is spiritually begotten from that higher power—the almighty and eternal Spirit of God. The Christ is a spiritual light who is born from eternal light and gives enlightenment to those who receive him.

"Begotten" can simply be defined as born or reborn (either from a male or female principal). Eternally begotten would imply that Christ is begotten without end. Where and how does this happen? This event happens in our world of time, in you and me, the people of God, when we are begotten, or born again, by the Holy Spirit, as Jesus was.

Quite often, we have heard Evangelicals speak of being "born again." It is rare that we hear a Catholics speak of this experience. We might wonder, What is this all about? Yet Jesus is placing much emphasis on this condition when he is speaking to Nicodemus in the third chapter of John, 1-12. *Now there was a Pharisee named Nicodemus, a ruler of the Jews. He came to Jesus at night and said to him, "Rabbi, we know that you are a teacher who has come from God, for no one can do these signs that you are doing unless God is with him." Jesus answered and said to him, "Amen, amen, I say to you, no one can see the kingdom of God without being born from above.* "Nicodemus does not understand what Jesus has said to him in spite of his religious education, and replies, *"How can a person once grown old be born again? Surely he cannot reenter his mother's womb and be born again, can he? Jesus answered, Amen, amen, I say to you, no one can enter the kingdom of God without being born of water and Spirit. What is born of flesh is flesh and what is born of spirit is spirit. Do not be amazed that I told you, 'You must be born from above.' The wind blows where it wills, and you can hear the sound it makes but you do not know where it comes from or where it goes; so it is with everyone who is born of the Spirit."* Nicodemus answered and said to him, *"How can this happen?"* By this time, Jesus must be a bit frustrated with a teacher of Israel who is ignorant of spiritual matters, and he reemphasizes his statement for the **third time**. *Jesus answered and said to him. "You are a teacher of Israel and you do not understand this? Amen, amen, I say to you, we speak of what we know and we testify to what we have seen,* (Jesus is testifying to his own experience.) *but you people do not accept our testimony. If I tell you about earthly things and you do not believe, how will you believe if I tell you about heavenly things?"*

Jesus is clearly telling Nicodemus (**three times**) that he must have a spiritual rebirth, which can only come from above.

Jesus knows and has revealed his own **experience** to Nicodemus because Jesus himself is begotten from above. He is able to reveal what the kingdom is like, what one can *see and do* when born of the Spirit. He performs signs and wonders, speaks with wisdom under the inspiration of the Spirit, moves hearts and minds of the rich and poor, teaches the illiterate, adults, and children, women and men. His words are with compassion and instructions of love. His followers must have been filled with joy as they listened to the Sermon on the Mount. Who had ever spoken this way before?

Scripture tells us that Jesus grew in the knowledge and wisdom of God, but there was also that all-at-once experience in the river Jordan. The Holy Spirit was working in Jesus throughout his natural life (as it has been working in the natural life of all of us), but also in that extraordinary way when The Spirit of God, that heavenly higher power came to dwell upon, and within Jesus, as he was begotten from above and anointed the Christ.

A beautiful lesson is given to us in this third chapter of John. What are we to learn from it? How are we to understand what Jesus the Christ is *testifying* to? How are we to accept his *testimony?* One way to know is, believe with faith what Christ has taught us, and another way is to have the **experience** of the anointed one and be born again from above. How can we have this experience, and, do we want to have the experience of knowing Christ within us?

When Jesus went to the synagogue in Nazareth, he read from the scroll of Isaiah where it was written: *"The Spirit of the Lord is upon me, because he has anointed me to bring glad tidings to the poor. He has sent me to proclaim liberty to captives and recovery of sight to the blind, to let the oppressed go free, and to proclaim a year acceptable to the Lord." (Luke 4, 18-19)* Jesus is giving witness about himself as, *He said to them, "Today this scripture passage is fulfilled in your hearing." (Luke 4, 21)* Jesus is letting everyone know that he, the anointed one, like Isaiah, is also the liberator.

In the Gospel of Luke chapter 3, verse 16, John the Baptist tells us what Jesus will do for us; ***"He will baptize you with the Holy Spirit and fire."*** The baptism of fire is the fire of love, which is the spirit of anointing which came upon the apostles and disciples at Pentecost, like a strong driving wind, and it will come upon all who follow the way that Jesus taught. Will we allow ourselves to be touched by this awesome fire? This fire gives light to enlighten and guide. This fire burns as only love can burn. This fire of love is the most contagious spirit that God has bestowed upon the human race and all of creation. To accept what Christ has to offer us it is necessary to experience the *water,* the *wind,* and the *fire,* again and again.

"The Christ" is eternally *begotten* in all those who accept him because of Jesus—God's gift—who has shown us *the way* to be anointed by the Spirit, to become another Christ, and to participate in his priesthood. When we personally accept Jesus Christ into our lives, we become one with his spirit and share personal experiences with each other.

"He came to what was his own, (the Jewish people) *but his own people did not accept him. But to those who did accept him he gave power to become children of God, to those who believe in his name, who were born not by natural generation nor by human choice nor by man's decision but of God." (Jn 1:11-12).* Like

Jesus, Son of God we are to be God's children, anointed, begotten from above, sons and daughters, other Christ's, as we accept Jesus the Christ as our own.

Peter tells us: *"But you are a chosen race,* (The Jewish people were called the chosen race. Now, Peter is saying that Christ's followers, are a chosen race.) *a royal priesthood,* (because we share in the priesthood of Christ.) **a holy nation,** (because we are the people of God,) *a people of his own, so that you may announce the praises of him who called you out of darkness into his wonderful light. "* (One Peter 2:9) Being in this "wonderful light" brings enlightenment, with all blessings that Peter mentions. We belong to him. He takes possession of us and we claim him as our own. When this happens, we certainly want to announce the praises of God and tell of his wonderful ways.

At the water baptism of every Christian, the first step is taken toward our rebirth, (by someone who spoke for us). At the confirmation of every Christian, the adult must speak for him/herself. There must be a conscious desire and commitment to Christ and his way. This should be the new Pentecost in which the Christian can be "born from above." This should have happened at our Confirmation, or perhaps at a Charismatic prayer meeting. It can happen to anyone at any time, here and now. Remember, "The wind blows where it will." Christ has planned this experience for those who follow his way. This was his promise to his apostles and disciples. This is *the promise kept* when all those in "the upper room" received the Holy Spirit and were begotten from above. People need to know and **will** what they are doing, experience the Spirit of Christ and not just go through a ritual. To be born from above is to know Christ personally, to be in relationship with him and ultimately be in union with him—*to be one-with-him.*

It is important to know that this experience is possible! To speak of a "born again" *experience* in Catholic tradition has not been a practice, and one can only wonder, why? I have *never* heard a sermon or homily on the subject of being "born again" or "begotten from above" in the Catholic Church during my lifetime!

It is out of my personal experiences during these past forty years that sometimes I have witnessed fear in clergymen, sometimes bewilderment or even disbelief when I have spoken of spiritual matters. I believe there are good men in the Church serving God, but I have questioned—are some like Nicodemus, searching their hearts, and wondering . . . ?

Yet I thank God for those priests who have experienced a rebirth from above, for in truth, this is the experience of the *priesthood of Christ*, the anointed, begotten from above, *eternal one* who can say, "*before Abraham came to be, I AM.*" *(Jn 8:58)* (The eternal mind of God is speaking through Jesus the Christ.)

Jesus has often reminded us, "*For behold, the kingdom of God is among you.*" *(or, within you) (Lk 17:21)* We need to know of this wonder, and partake of the grace that God will release for us as we ask forgiveness for our offences, and commit our love to him.

Jesus said to the Pharisees, "*Woe to you, scholars of the law! You have taken away the key of knowledge. You yourselves did not enter and you stopped those trying to enter*" *(Lk11:52)* Perhaps unwittingly our leaders have done the same to the people of God. Some of our shepherds have lost their way, and it is only with the help of the Holy Spirit that the key of knowledge will be recovered. **The way** that Jesus Christ revealed is now being renewed in his people.

In One John 2:27, we are told, "*As for you, the anointing that you received from him remains in you, so that you do not need anyone to teach you. But his anointing teaches you about everything and is true and not false; just as it taught you, remain in him.*"

Paul tells us that in Christ there is neither male nor female. It is apparent that to him, when he speaks of Christ, he is speaking of Spirit. The Body of Christ, which we are, is both male and female. Again, in the Spirit of Christ, women, the other half of God's image, as well as men, are in Christ too, and participate in the priesthood of Christ, along with men.

Under the influence of the Holy Spirit, good Pope John set the Spirit of Christ free for the people of God. It is up to us, the people of God, (the chosen race) to keep the Spirit free, maintain our faith and love for the Body of Christ, and awaken our spirituality afresh. We must recover the key of knowledge and unlock the treasures that are in store for the people of God.

What happens when a person receives an *anointing* from the Holy Spirit? First, a transformation within the person takes place. It causes a very great *awareness of the presence* of God within one's self and others, about everything created and uncreated. The insight with this new awareness elevates all of creation to a spiritual level. You begin to see yourself and the world differently. Enlightenment enters in and makes all things *new*. One is brought into union with God, and there is constant discovery of the One who has become your very self. To discover your *self* is to discover God. The person who is newly born into this spiritual life is truly a child of God, a new son, a new daughter, with all the privileges, gifts, blessings, and even sufferings that a son or daughter of the Father accepts for the continuation of *the way* that Jesus has taught. Like Jesus, you will be led into the desert where God will speak to your heart.

Jesus said, *"The Advocate, the holy Spirit that the Father will send in my name—he will teach you everything and remind you of all that [I] have told you." (John 14:26)*

A rebirth from above is to *"put on the new self" (Eph4:24)* (as Paul tells us) i.e., the Spirit of Christ. His Spirit lives and acts in us. He gives new life, eternal life, where we can say with Christ, in God, I AM, and there is no death for one who has eternal life. Enlightenment is given to "see" clearly with a new Spirit—Christ's own love of God—the Holy Spirit, *love of humankind and all of creation*—all anew. *"So whoever is in Christ is a new creation: the old things have passed away; behold, new things have come." (Two Corinthians 5:17)* Here we are drawn into eternal life, even while we live in the world. With all the newness comes revelations and visions, gifts of the Holy Spirit, knowledge of God, and discovery of *self*, the universe and kingdom within. This is a resurrection to new life (as Saint Paul says), where the corruptible is clothed with incorruptibility and the mortal with immortality. *This is an extraordinary event.* In our rebirth, our old self has died with Christ, and a new self is raised up, not just in Christ, but as Christ, who comes again and again in each of us. Are you looking forward to the Coming of Christ? Look for it within yourselves.

How can this be possible for the people of God? God is a giver and a lover of all his creation! He loves every one of us unconditionally and desires to have us share fully in his life. One must *ask, from the heart*—believe, as with the innocence of a child; and the Eternal One will *bring forth* the eternally begotten one in all who welcome His *Coming again. "Ask and you will receive; seek and you will find; knock and the door will be opened to you." (Lk 11:9)*

My experience of being begotten from above urges me on with a great desire to reintroduce this experiential knowledge of God, Father, Son and Holy Spirit to the people of God, people whom I know and love, people whom God knows and loves. It is a gift of God waiting to be accepted. The early Christians knew this experience very well. Today, Christians and all people of the earth are invited to experience the coming of Christ again into each and every life, in mind, body and spirit.

An experience:
You have heard . . . God comes to us at the point of our need. Long ago I had a special need and prayed about it from the depths of my heart. Something within began to change. That was more than forty years ago. I went to speak with a priest about an extraordinary change that was taking place in my thinking. Enlightenment was coming upon me. (I did not realize what was happening to me at that time.) As I spoke, relating the events of my new thinking, he began to cry. Thinking that I had said something wrong, I asked, "Why are you crying?" "You have seen God", he said. Shaking my head in disbelief I said, "I have seen his love." "God is Love" he said. For the first time in my life, at the age or twenty-seven, I had heard, "God is Love"! (Why had no one told me this before?) After a while I bought a Bible from him. I began to read it. (Something I had previously been forbidden to do) The Holy Spirit began to give new life to ancient words! In church, the scriptures were being read in English! They suddenly became living, meaningful words.

Then the floodgates of heaven were opened! God is Love! But Love is everywhere! The honeymoon began. I began to KNOW God! And in knowing God, his greatness, his goodness, his love and beauty, one becomes humbled, even humiliated by ones sinfulness, and the recognition of one's littleness. There was an immediate prayer in asking forgiveness for my sins. Then with repentance, a blessing,—an anointing!

I was saying an Act of Contrition as I was sweeping the floor in the living room when the Spirit of God came upon me. There I stood, motionless, as wave upon wave of that overwhelming Presence of God moved upon me, from the top of my head down though my entire body and into my feet. I cannot say how long it lasted, perhaps several minutes. The experience left me speechless and joyful. It left me with a sense of euphoria for that entire day and many days thereafter. What was experienced then is what Jesus spoke to Nicodemus about, *"Amen, Amen I say to you, no one can enter the kingdom of God without being born from above." ". . . no one can enter the kingdom of God without being born of water and Spirit (Jn 3:3,5).* And again John the Baptist says of Jesus, *"He will baptize you with the Holy Spirit and fire." (Mt 3:11)*

For this and many outstanding experiences, I praise and thank God. *I have done nothing to merit this blessing.* It is a gift from the grace of God. It is what Jesus has willed for each one of us. It is the plan of our Father for his people. I pray for this blessing to be upon every one of the people of God.

I encourage both women and men to accept the anointing that should be yours, as the Holy Spirit enlightens you. Please God that you have this experience. Those who have been called must persevere in the Word as revealed in scripture. It is the Word of the Lord that must have our strict attention and this is what we have put our faith in. What I state is true. The people of God must have a clear understanding of the meaning of the word, Christ. It was only a few weeks ago that I heard an educated Catholic man,—a politician, declare on a TV news program that the reason that women can never be priests is that Christ was a man. He has never been educated to the fact that Christ is a Spirit of anointing,—neither male nor female. St. Paul tells us this fact in many ways, and so do Peter and John. Christ is the anointed and enlightened one.

Those who are called and have the anointing of the Holy Spirit will in conscience, courageously claim the priesthood of Christ and will be sent with the gifts and blessings of God for the New Reign of God that is upon us.

2000

revised 2006
Biblical quotes are from the New American Bible.

IV

The Coming of Christ

What can be said about the end of the world, the end of time, the coming of Christ again and the beginning of a new age? How is this to be understood? There are a few insights given to us from the Bible. *"Behold I am with you always, even until the end of the age."* (Mt 28:20) Here Jesus is speaking of his spirit that would be with us in a limited way until the end of the age, for his body died, resurrected, and ascended to heaven, but he made a promise: *"If you love me, you will keep my commandments. And I will ask the Father, and he will give you another Advocate to be with you always, the Spirit of Truth, which the world cannot accept, because it neither sees nor knows it. But you know it because it remains with you, and will be in you. I will not leave you orphans; I will come to you. In a little while the world will no longer see me, but you will see me because I live and you will live. On that day you will realize that I am in my Father and you are in me and I in you"* (Jn 14:15-20). Jesus is revealing the trinity and the gift of wholeness to those who accept the Advocate.

At Pentecost the *Spirit of Christ returned to those who believed.* The Spirit of Christ continues to come to those who believe, and when it does, an *end comes* into their lives, for they are *begotten from above*, and *new life begins* for that person. There is an end of the old and a beginning of the new. Death and sin no longer hold power over such a person. The apostles and Paul knew this experience well (though I am not sure they had full comprehension of their experience, for Paul was urging single people not to marry, believing that Christ would come again very soon). And all the while, Christ was continually coming into their lives. A mystical death had taken place. This was again evident when Paul spoke of himself in the third person, *"I know someone in Christ who, fourteen years ago [whether in the body or out of the body I do not know, God knows], was caught up to the third heaven. And I know that this person [whether in the body or out of the body I do not know, God knows] was caught up into*

Paradise and heard ineffable things, which no one may utter (2 Corinthians 12,2-4). Christ's coming happened in Paul's life in many different ways, as it can and does for all of us.

"The End," the coming of Christ, is happening continually, just as a new beginning is happening continually. While alive in the human body, one can die a death to the body, because the person is reborn in the Spirit of Christ. Paul in One Corinthians 15: 42-44, speaks of this event in another way,—as a resurrection experience. *"So also in the resurrection of the dead. It is sown corruptible; it is raised incorruptible. It is sown dishonorable; it is raised glorious. It is sown weak; it is raised powerful. It is sown a natural body; it is raised a spiritual body. If there is a natural body, there is also a spiritual one."* This is the reward for being in union with Christ and his Love. Love is the force, the energy, the gift and the power that can say, as Christ does in Revelations 21:5, 6; *"Behold I make all things new." "I [am] the Alpha and the Omega, the beginning and the end."* When there is an *end*, there is always a *new* beginning. God always begins at the end. And at the edge of the universe, there is an eternal springtime for God. *Love is the key* to new life, new beginnings, and new freedom. Love is a gift. Acceptance is what needs to be learned while in the body—living expectantly of his coming again, though it may cause distress and pain. Anyone living with that "expectation" will be recalling the words of Christ: "There will be earthquakes in various places . . ." These and similar words of Christ play in the psyche. But those things too "pass away," and we hear, *"Death is swallowed up in victory. Where, O death, is your victory? Where, O death, is your sting!" (1Cor.15:55)*

Christ is forever coming, while we are in the flesh or spirit, when we live and when we die, when in joy or when in pain, when we sin and when we recover from sin, while we wait . . . and while we know that he has come. He is NOW! The rewards of his coming are his love and his freedom . . . gifts given to the little ones—those wise enough to accept.

The new millennium brings a new age, a freedom waiting to be accepted, where the spirit and the flesh will not be at war or oppose one another (as we previously had been taught). But the spirit and the flesh will complement one another and be at peace and unity with one another, for the flesh is holy as the spirit is holy! *In truth the essence of flesh is spirit.*

It is sad to reflect on the past, primarily seeing "virgins and martyrs" as *the* only holy people. What hope was there for married people, human beings who loved each other, who were not given to understand that their lovemaking was holy? *Where* are "Mr. and Mrs. Holy Persons" in the institutional church? Who could think that they may have had the experience of the spirit and ecstasy and presence of God in their sexual love—who could believe it! Unfortunate is the thinking that would believe otherwise!

While the teaching church has placed much (too much) emphasis on celibacy and virginity, it seems to have failed to give notice or recognition to the *presence* and activity of God in a sexual union of a man and a woman, affirming the profoundly personal intimate relationship between God (who produces the ecstasy) and human beings who love one another. And not only in sexual union, but people who love each other can also know *this presence* which gives that similar ecstasy even though they may be across the room from one another. It seems that the love relationship between a man and a woman is the perfect image of the relationship happening between our Father and his Love—the Holy Spirit. Those to whom the *presence* of *divine love* is given, they are the ones who will know it. *Christ comes* in ways that only those who experience it can recognize. The church cannot confine the experience of God to the *religious* life or celibate people. There is an end also to some beliefs, only to open fuller truth to new beliefs.

It is very evident to the practical and spiritually minded people who live in the new millennium—the voices of all *the people of God*, including women and married people (whether clergy or laity), will give a more inclusive contribution to the Body of Christ than just a celibate clergy can. What will the transfiguration of the world be like, from the old to the new? In the End, God, who makes all things *new*, will bestow divine love upon the children in this new age. Democracy, freedom, equality, justice, peace, wisdom and love will be the rule of God's Reign. We will be subjects of royalty, with the knowledge of God our creator—Father and the love of the Holy Spirit, our Mother—prime mover.

Maranatha!

1999

V

Reflections on the Gospel of John

"*In the beginning was the Word, and the Word was with God, and the Word was God. He was in the beginning with God. All things came to be through him, and without him nothing came to be. What came to be through him was life, and this life was the light of the human race; the light shines in the darkness, and the darkness has not overcome it*" *(John 1:1-5)*.

These highly symbolic words from John are as beautiful and timely today as they were the day they were written. The "Word," who is Christ, was with God, our Father and creator, not just from the beginning (when we speak of time) but before the beginning, as Jesus Christ testifies, "*I AM,*" *(Jn8:58)* which means, I AM before *anything* came to be, I AM even after everything has been. He is the *existence* for and of God our Father and Mother. And what is the purpose of this existence? It is *to be*. And this *Being* is moved, motivated, and inhabited by the Father-Creator and Love, his Holy Spirit, our Mother. All of creation can only *be*, and not *do*, except for the love (will) of God. *Existence can only be. The Holy Spirit (will or love) animates the knowledge of our Father-Creator in existence, their Son.*

What came *to be* through him was *life,* and there is only life in *existence* because the Spirit gives it life. To speak of this in a different way, we might say that the Word is the knowingness or knowledge of God the Father, which came *to be* in the Son by the action (will) and power of the Holy Spirit. Then the question is asked, *what is existence* that can only *be?* Does it have composition, mass? Does it have energy? The answer to these questions is yes. The *existence* of created life is matter, composed of the elements and the energy contained in them. This I believe: that God is energy, moving with love and knowledge in our world and in our human condition. It is more apparent now than ever before that humankind has been given much knowledge and much power over the very elements that God has created for the good all. One cannot help but wonder how vulnerable God is in his creation because of his love—giving himself, his life, completely, as Jesus did on the cross. Now what will humankind do with the world of God, the birthplace of Jesus the Christ his son?

"He was in the world, and the world came to be through him, but the world did not know him. He came to what was his own, but his own people did not accept him. But to those who did accept him he gave power to become children of God, to those who believe in his name, who were born not by natural generation nor by human choice nor by a man's decision but of God" (John 1:10-13). How can it be that people do not, or cannot, recognize Christ in the world? Who has failed in letting him be known? Is it the fault of persons or systems or organizations? Could it be that God himself will and must make himself obvious to those yet unable to see? Could it be that the Creator is still in the process of creating and it will take *time* for him to reveal himself through the revelation of evolution? Could it be that his Spirit of love—given in the Spirit of Christ—will grow greater and at an accelerated pace as the world of people evolve into the enlightened children of God? The true light, which enlightens everyone, has come and will continuously come, again and again, into the world. *"What is born of flesh is flesh and what is born of spirit is spirit. (John 3:6)*

In truth, I can testify to this experience. It is not my experience alone. I boldly state that it is our Father and the Holy Spirit who testify through this Christ in *existence.* There is a world of people who have come to know the Spirit of Christ in their lives. This experience will continue as long as there is a world and people who live in it.

"I am the light of the world. Whoever follows me will not walk in darkness, but will have the light of life." (John 8:12). The divine Christ is speaking here. The light that he is speaking of is the enlightenment that he (is) has from the Holy Spirit. This light is what he desires to give to his followers in order that they—we—will walk in the light (enlightenment) with him. The light of Christ brings wisdom, and wisdom is the beginning of knowledge. It is difficult to know the fullness of what God has to reveal to us his children without experiencing the light of Christ within. Those with enlightenment are able to see Christ in all the enlightened ones in all religions of the earth.

John's gospel speaks strongly in symbols, as Jesus himself does—the word, the light, darkness, water, bread of life, being born of water and spirit, born from above; and these symbols are just human words attempting to express a higher reality, a spiritual reality—Jesus the Christ, John the Mystic—trying to convey the divine to the human, the human to the divine.

In the Book of Glory, Jesus continues to instruct his disciples and remains true to his teachings. He prepares to wash the feet of the disciples but meets resistance. Peter insists that Jesus should not wash his feet. Peter wasn't listening when Jesus said that the first shall be last and the last shall be first or he who humbles himself shall be exalted and he who exalts himself will be humbled, or, do unto others as you would have them to unto you. So again, Jesus says, *"I have given you a model to follow, so that as I have done for you, you should also do," (Jn 13:14).* This model is not limited to the washing of feet. The whole life of Jesus is our model.

The discourses at the last supper are a revelation from the heart of Christ. Here he has reached into the depths of his being and is giving his life's energy and love, pouring out his very *self,* trying to inform the disciples of what is going to happen to him, trying to tell them of his very intimate relationship with God his Father. He is in *union* with his Father (the eternal knowingness), letting them know that they too can be in union with the Father and him. But first he must go in order that the Advocate, the Spirit of truth will come, and they will be able to *see* and *know.*

How true to his words, for after his death, love and the Spirit of truth descended upon the followers of Jesus the Christ. In the new light, which was given to them, they, as well as we, can say along with him, *from the beginning,* "I Am . . ."

Reflecting further on the gospel of John, with so many personal discourses attributed to Jesus, one cannot help but think that the Spirit of Christ was speaking *through* John himself, bringing to mind all that was taught by Jesus, including the fact that he sent the Paraclete as promised and brought all these things to the mind of John. We shall all be taught by God.

March 19, 1999

VI

Where Can We Find the Christ?

"Jesus 2000" was the title given to the art competition that was sponsored by the *National Catholic Reporter* in 1999. There were over sixteen hundred representations of Jesus Christ from one thousand four artists in nineteen countries. Panels of judges, along with Sister Wendy Beckett, a famed BBC art expert, were to choose the winners. A winner was chosen, and a booklet of about sixty works of art on the person of "Jesus 2000" was published and distributed with the December 24, 1999, issue of the *National Catholic Reporter*.

The art painting of "Jesus 2000" that took first prize was that of a young black person dressed in the garments of the Dominican order. This was considered the valid prize winning portrayal of Jesus today.

As one turns the pages of the booklet, the pictures reveal one starving and naked human being trying to feed another starving and naked human being. Yes, I believe it is easy enough to see Jesus in the hungry people of the earth. This is how Mother Teresa often saw him. *"Whatever you did for one of these least brothers of mine, you did for me." (Mt25:40)*. There was a picture of the beautiful Mystic Christ. He was a great spirit of a man anchored in the waters of earth. Buffaloes and the prairies passed over his legs. A fig leaf was well placed and a loaf of bread was in his abdomen. Wheat and grapes in his arms, the mountains were there at his heart. His shoulders and head were in the clouds and sky, among the stars of the heavens. This is how another artist is apparently portraying Christ—a spirit larger than the physical person of Jesus. (I really liked this one.)

Then there was the picture of a woman, dark skinned and with a serious expression on her face and a headband in her hair. Could Christ be a woman today? *"For all of you who were baptized into Christ have clothed yourself with*

Christ. There is neither Jew nor Greek, there is neither slave nor free person, there is not male and female; for you are all one in Christ Jesus." (Gal 3: 27-28). Could this woman bring forth Christ in her life and to the world today? By faith, we can believe this is possible. Is Christ hiding or being revealed in these paintings—in these people? Has Christ been confined to a person of two thousand years ago or to the tabernacles of our churches, or is Christ a spirit that is alive in people and in the creations of our Father?

The words of St. Paul come to mind: *"For in one Spirit we were all baptized into one body, whether Jew or Greek, slaves or free persons, and we were all given to drink of one Spirit."* (1 Cor 12:13) Paul is telling us that the Spirit of Christ has united a *body of people* together, and *his Spirit*, the Omega Spirit, has been given to us his people, if we will accept it, from the day of Pentecost until this very day. How many Christians believe that Christ lives in all of us, even in Jesus 2000?

In the January 21, 2000, issue of *NCR*, there were letters that spoke of how Catholics see or do not see Jesus Christ today.

One woman was content to see Jesus as is captured on the shroud of Turin. A retired police officer felt sure that he had arrested the individual in this picture or someone who looked like him many times during the past twenty years. He was certain that this was not the image of Jesus and he was sure it was not the image that thousands of other people had of Jesus either. Someone declared that the picture should be destroyed because it did not depict the true Jesus, according to the teachings of the Catholic Church. Another person stated that the picture should have been called, Truth. An African American person thought it was magnificent. One woman stated that she was filled with shock and disgust about the new Jesus and decided never to go into a Catholic Church again.

It was with dismay that I read the many unfavorable letters with regard to the winning artwork of "Jesus 2000." After these two thousand years of Christianity, how is it possible that so many of God's people have such a limited understanding of Jesus the Christ? Would the reaction to this artwork have been any different if the title of the contest had been, "Christ 2000"?

There were twenty-seven unfavorable letters and twenty favorable letters to *NCR* in the January 21st, 2000 issue with regard to the "Jesus 2000" art competition. These questions now arise. What impressions have Catholics received from the teaching Church with regard to who Jesus Christ is and what he has done and given to us? Have Catholics really received the Good News? If not, why not? This is of major importance, especially since Catholics are given so much information by way of rules, regulations, encyclicals, documents, declarations and demands. Yet the important and necessary teachings about Jesus the Christ is evidently neglected. How long before the people of God will be given the good news about our Christ? This is an important spiritual and moral matter.

It is written in the Gospel of John many times, and the other gospels too, and the Acts of the Apostles: *"Whoever loves me will keep my word, and my Father will love him, and we will come to him and make our dwelling with him."* *(Jn14:23)* Again, there is the prayer of Jesus Christ for all believers, all who have been, and will be baptized in the Christian faith. *"I pray not only for them, but also for those who will believe in me through their word, so that they may all be one, as you, Father, are in me and I in you, that they also may be in us, that the world may believe that you sent me" (Jn 17:20-21). "Remain in me, as I remain in you. I am the vine, you are the branches. Whoever remains in me and I in him will bear much fruit (Jn 15:4,5).* How plainly can Jesus the Christ let us know that he has given himself to us, in spirit and truth, and that he lives in us! How many times and how many ways does Christ need to tell us that he lives in us? But do we believe and accept this fact? This is GOOD NEWS! By the grace of God, the Spirit of Christ lives in us. Christ, "The way, the truth, and the life," is a gift that brings us liberation from evil and opens the gates to the New Reign of God.

Why do we love him? Isn't it because he is the most
loving, compassionate and moral person who has ever lived
in our world? Isn't it because of the character, qualities
and values he possesses, reveals, and teaches? Can we see these
truths of Christ in people of black, white, yellow, and
red skin? Can we look beyond color and see the *spirit
of the person*—the Spirit of Christ?

We who have been baptized into Christ have been given his spirit and anointing. That which has been revealed about him makes him *our hero*—a person we wish to imitate and become. That which we love about him is the quality and character of the man, for he is full of courage and virtue. We adore and worship this God-man, Jesus the Christ. He disperses his spirit—LOVE, and fills us with hope, and the faith we once had has now become sure knowledge. Those who have his spirit live with his energy, which generates strength to persevere in truth with the *gifts* that he lives and gives; wisdom, understanding, prudence, knowledge, justice, humility, reverence, piety and respect for God and man. He is merciful and compassionate. We are *forced to love* the virtue and goodness of this man, Jesus Christ, imitating the qualities and character of his person as we participate in his spirit. *We live in him. He lives in us.* We are ONE in the Spirit of Christ.

Where is Christ 2000? He's not in hiding! He is continually revealing himself to his people, men and women, in different ways at different times—in art, literature, poems, people, nature, song—all of life, especially in love. And if Christ is ever going to *come again* (and we believe this truth), let's tell it like it is and *accept Christ's Spirit* as is. Let us not delay the Parousia. The people of God deserve to hear, believe, and live the Good News for the sake of the Reign of God.

We must believe that Jesus the Christ is the anointed of God and lives in all of us, regardless of color or gender. It *began* with our baptism!

2000

VII

The Word Became Flesh

Mary and Joseph could not find a place that would offer comfort, warmth or security in their time of need. There was only a stable where animals were sheltered—a primitive place to give birth to a child. One can only wonder why God allowed his Word to begin in such a lowly place. But Mary proved to be a strong vessel and accepting of the most humble circumstances that God could ever place anyone in. She was glad to rest, have a little privacy and find some protection from the unfriendly elements. Like all women before and after her who ever gave birth to a child, she labored in bearing new life. From the body of a young woman, in a very natural way, a baby boy was born amid the water and blood that flowed from the body of this new mother, Mary. The baby was given the name Jesus as an angel had foretold.

Who is more helpless than a baby or a little child, so very dependent upon the love and care of another? God became helpless and dependent when he took form in the flesh of Jesus. God in his helplessness also put trust in two human beings, Mary and Joseph, to love and nurture the child who would become the God-man. Jesus grew in his awareness, and with the enlightenment of a prophet knew that God his heavenly Father was depending on him to carry out a plan that would reveal to the world the way to the kingdom. It would also reveal that Jesus would be the anointed Son of God—the Christ who would change the world. What a responsibility Jesus accepted. How could he possibly do all that would be required of him? He knew the fate of the prophets. He knew the limitations and weakness of the flesh. His gifts, his love, his endurance and perseverance would be tested beyond measure. He would not only need to lead the way in guiding peoples and nations, but in accomplishing all this, he would teach his followers to *become* like him—other Christs, for he is the *firstborn* of all who follow. Christ is the *pearl* purchased at a great price. The *way* was revealed. He would never be just an ordinary human being. He became a super human being, that is, divine. All that he did, he did from his human body, but his indomitable spirit came from within the heart and love of a wondrous and mysterious God. Was Jesus the Messiah the moment he was conceived, or the moment he was born, or when, as a young boy, he conversed with the learned men in the temple? To be sure, Jesus was predestined from all eternity to *become* the Christ and Messiah for all the people of God.

At about the age of twelve, something special happens to human beings. God has designed these events in males and females of our species. We know that body chemistry begins to change, and perhaps with that is the first conscious touch of the spirit beginning to emerge. Jesus, at this age, experienced something special, and it would stay with him and grow in him thereafter. Jesus was *becoming* the Christ. At the Jordan River, Jesus was not just baptized with water. The *Holy Spirit gave birth to the Christ.* Jesus was born again—anointed the Christ. *"What is born of flesh is flesh, and what is born of spirit is spirit"* (John, 3:6).

God has a message here for the helpless, the poor, and those who come into the world in unfavorable circumstances, whether it is Bethlehem, Darfur or Detroit. From lowly places he raises up those he loves to great heights. He reveals the processes through which life takes us. And when we accept his grace, we evolve most favorably in the way that Jesus came to know in his life. Through his experiences and examples he has taught us how to walk on our path through life.

Human experiences, working, loving, caring, sharing joy and pain, observing nature of every kind, the beauty of the earth and sky, the cycle of the seasons, birth and death, and the everyday toil of human beings with the energy of God at work within their bodies are all marvels to be wondered at. The parables of Jesus are full of his *experiences.* There are stories about fishermen, shepherds, wheat fields and vineyards, self-willed people, generous fathers, selfish sons, women who were treated as less than human, faithful and unfaithful servants, and the mercy and generosity of a personal God. The human senses of Jesus were stretched to the limit. He never stopped listening, watching, learning, loving, teaching. He became wise, for he had used all the faculties that God his Father had given him. He was filled with grace by the power of the

Holy Spirit and was begotten from above, filled with enlightenment and became The Christ.

There probably are many ways to describe "Christ." John the apostle speaks of the "Word" that was in the beginning. He is speaking of an eternal Spirit, which, for a very short time, took the form of flesh. And this *seed* of flesh—this single cell of cosmic spiritual energy, was planted in the creation of our Creator-Father. In *time* it grew, in the womb of a human woman, was born in a natural way, evolved into a loving reflective person who came to be one with *Being*, knew his human and divine nature, and could claim the title, son of man and son God. His mind was one with the Father, who is *all-knowing*, his spirit was one with the Holy Spirit of God, his Mother who is *all-loving*

"Amen, amen, I say to you, unless the grain of wheat falls to the ground and dies, it remains just a grain of wheat; but if it dies, it produces much fruit" (Jn 12:24). Jesus the Christ truly was speaking of himself, the grain of wheat—that seed from heaven who died and was buried in the earth. Jesus is the seed of the Father in which the Spirit of Christ took root for the purpose of fulfilling the Father's plan. This plan reveals the way to the Kingdom. Christ rose up to new life with an ever-increasing, powerful spirit. It touched this one and that one and everyone. The *Spirit of Christ* now grows everywhere, evolving, becoming cosmic in the consciousness of God's people.

The oneness that Jesus the Christ came to know with the Father was that he *knew* he preexisted from all eternity. *"Amen, amen, I say to you, before Abraham came to be, I AM" (Jn 8:58)*

And again, *"Believe me that I Am in the Father and the Father is in me . . . (Jn 14:11)"* Jesus is at the omega point in his life, completely one with the Father and the Holy Spirit. For again he states, *"I will ask the Father, and he will send you another advocate to be with you always, the Spirit of truth . . . (Jn 14:16)."* The Trinity was whole and complete in the person of Jesus the Christ. He was the omega person, one in *being* with God the Father and Holy Spirit.

This is the benefit of the Pascal Mystery—that Spirit of Christ, which was planted in a cell of flesh, in the person of Jesus, died; from that, his great and wonderful spirit would grow. It is a fertile and contagious spirit; one cell of flesh after another, century after century, has caught fire from the Spirit of Christ, and all the cells of flesh in the world combine to make up the growing Body of Christ, from the time of the first ray of consciousness in human beings until time is no more. His Spirit is alive and well. The awareness—this reflective consciousness in his people, is Christ looking at his coming again and again. It is a hard-won and greatly appreciated prize and gift.

God is still helpless and dependent in the flesh of his people today. God is depending on his people to bring forth the Christ in our lives. For this is what we have been taught to do. Will we accept . . . ? Have we known that the Spirit of Christ who lived in Jesus, is the same Christ who is designed to live and love in each one of us? Will we be fertile soil for the seed of his Spirit to grow and mature in? He has died to live in us. The Spirit of Christ is free for all.

We must praise and thank Jesus the Christ with an eternal thank you from the depths of our *being* for all that he has given to us—his life!

VIII

Genesis Again

In the first story of Genesis, the writer is caught up in the wonder of creation, imagining how it all began. He starts by going back to the beginning of time and writes about how God created the heavens and the earth. He arranges an order in which events happen and growth occurs. The man looks at everything and writes, "God saw how good it was." Then God said, *"Let us make man in our image, after our likeness." "God created man in his image, **in the divine image** he created him; male and female he created them." (Genesis 1: 26, 27).* It is important not to overlook the inspired words of this author, noting that the female is in the divine image as well as the male. More often than not it is good to contemplate the feminine of God. This writer of Genesis did not tell us about *the fall.*

Another writer came along to tell the story about creation in a similar way. With at least two stories very much alike, there is a realization that these stories are from the same source. These writers have been in touch with an *origin* that is always the same, even though it may be expressed in different ways.

We know that these stories are "myth"; but how did it come to be that each person who was apparently inspired to tell of creation tells this same *kind of* story about "the beginning"? And seeing that there was really no one around in the beginning who could write such a story, how did it happen?

Having experienced something similar as the writers of Genesis, and having recorded it, an idea has occurred to me with regard to this. That there is a cosmic consciousness in our world, which otherwise might be called the mind of God, is apparent to me. This consciousness is touched by ordinary people who think about the world, its beauty and wonder, and how it came to be. This is only *a beginning* for the person who wishes to know and love more of what can be revealed. It is an alpha point of God revealing himself to humankind.

Another story tells us a little more about the man and woman that God created like himself. They lived in a garden of plenty where all was well and good. And they were as innocent as new babes. Curiously, a tree there bore fruit that could make the woman and man like God—knowing good and evil. That fruit was forbidden of them to eat, for if they did, their eyes would be opened. Nevertheless, they ate. Suddenly, there was a change. This man and woman saw each other naked. They had a need to cover themselves. Did they see their nakedness as bad or evil when their eyes were opened? (Does this attitude prevail to this day?)

Other questions arise about this beginning. We know this story is a myth, yet *it recurs in many of the world's religions in one form or another.* Can we conclude that all of these "beginning" stories come from the one source, or origin, whose consciousness becomes active in the minds of human beings who seek to discover this source of life that we otherwise call God?

The Garden of Eden story continues to be given and accepted by human beings throughout time. What could be the mystical story behind the myth? I shall present a poem on the subject and leave it up to the reader to discover if it is myth and/or mystical.

The Fall? Or The Beginning of Creation

Paradise is alive in boundless space
Loving To Know . . . is a beautiful life.
A new seed settled on an infinite garden,
and conception of existence again conceived.
Love grew, knowing He, and
Their love was seen through eternity.
"Greater will To Be become.
I'll give To Know without end,
As much as Knowing will accept, and more!"
So it was
Love gave and gave To Know,

Until To Know gave way and
Took To Know what He could not give.
Heaven burst in a ball of flame
And rushed toward its endless death.
Beauty fell into a steaming mud globe
While Knowing turned to salt.
On sped Love without To Know
And stopped to shine at Her birth.
It happened a countless life ago,
That Woman who loved To Know . . . the Man,
Gave To Know more than Knowing could Love;
Thus took the Spirit from Man.
There in the sky She burns for To Know,
While His face now regards their existence.

Could this mythological *fall* have happened in the heavens? (Would science call it the big bang?) Dare we ask if it was the Creator who caused what human beings have called "original" sin? (Is a new myth appropriate at this time in the history of humankind?) If this is true, then we also know that God was willing to do something about it. God has proven himself virtuous in accepting the consequences of what has come about as a result of the *Act of Creation* through the person of his son, Jesus the Christ. Can *the fall* really be termed sin? Human tongue is limited in expressing such a point. But do human beings have the responsibility to become as virtuous as their Creator and **accept** creation as his Son Jesus Christ has?

Because of the way the stories are presented . . . in a sequential form, one cannot help but wonder if a Genesis writer today would speak in terms of "the big bang" or "evolution" as the method in which God creates, or would that cosmic consciousness present the "beginning" in the same way as it did in ancient times? Because of my own experience, I have to say the "beginning" may always be as it has been presented from what is the origin, but with an insight that predates time. This is an earlier and new view of Genesis. There will always be the alpha, and humankind is forever working and moving toward the omega. There is realization of the growth of knowledge on all fronts of human and worldly development, for there is a force, energy at work, revealing the promise of a new creation. Sciences, psychology, sociology, medicine, religion, spirituality, economics, ecology, and all forms of knowledge are becoming a "new garden" for human kind to live and play in. "The Tree" is not unlike the original. Its use can produce good or evil. The fruit of these labors of knowledge must be used with love, which in turn produces wisdom, and with all the consciousness of the mind of Christ.

After the fall, there was a promise. The Creator told the evil serpent, *"I will put enmity between you and the woman, and between your offspring and hers; He will strike at your head, while you strike at his heel." (Genesis 3, 15)* "He," being Christ, would strike the fatal blow to evil. When, where, and how is this done? Obviously, it happened with the person of Jesus Christ, who gave his life not only for us but also *to* us. The Spirit of Christ—the love, energy, knowledge, peace, and life of Christ is given to a world of God's people. His coming is present for all to accept. It is you and I, all of us together in this great wonderful cosmic Spirit of Christ who defeat evil by living out the good and positive message of life that is given to us by him. God is still working within and on his creation. Evolution is continuing. Everything and everyone is still in the process of becoming. The Creator is still at work within each one of us.

In making another point on this matter, a poem again follows. Again, we human beings may be putting words into God's mouth; after all, what can we do except speak in human terms with regard to that higher mystical reality.

Love's Will Is Done

"I will create with you," he said.
She birthed his world, he continues to head.
"Let there earth and water be.
And heavenly skies though eternity.
Let there be light both day and night.
Let there be tails and wings in flight.
Let there be plants in blankets of green
To cover the earth as crown to a queen.
Let there be men to be called my friends,
That they may share the love I bear."
His will is done.

"The men do fail to follow my way!
Oh how I crave that they be saved.
I'll send my Son, the heart of me."
Love said to him:
"Behold your handmaid, Lord,
I'll bear the Savior we wish to share.
Myself to him alone I trust,
So go and care I must."
His will is done.

The Savior has come.
He teaches mercy, kindness, strength,
He humbly gives us Love to drink.
Your will be done in heaven here,
That we may know your Love, not fear.
So it is my Spirit's felt—
The Love in the Son of the Lord—
My Mother.
His will is done.

What is being repeated here is the fact that God saves what he has created through Christ, who is in both Jesus and Mary, you and I, all peoples, particularly those who say, "Behold your handmaid, Lord, I'll bear the savior we wish to share." It is SHE who brings forth the Christ, humanly, spiritually, and cosmically. Our response in this Spirit is what brings about His coming again in our lives and in our world, building the Kingdom, here and now.

Note:	Knowing=To Know=Man/ Masculine of God		
•	Loving=To Love/Wills=Woman/ Feminine of God	Existence=Son	
•	Father Creator	Mother Spirit, Sanctifies	Son Redeems/liberates

IX

Truth

What is truth?

A good question—and I arrived at an answer long ago when another person asked me that same question. I immediately responded, "Truth is fact."

The answer is true for me, but it needed some explanation, which only would come in time, after much thought, considering that God is also Truth. Then I came across the word *milieu* in connection with Christ. I understand it as the Spirit of Christ living in a particular environment and setting. One is truly blessed if one has been given the gift and grace to **accept** the milieu into which life has thrust upon them.

It is a fact of life that we experience good and evil, pain and joy, the traumatic and exhilarating, the ups and downs. The facts of life can be extreme and often unbearable, whether they are positive or negative.

It is of Truth that I wish to speak, and it is difficult to express events in time and their relationship with the infinite.

In Revelations, 22:13, the Christ who is eternal and unchanging says, "*I am the Alpha and the Omega, the first and the last, the beginning and the end.*" Here he is speaking in time so he uses words that describe limitations (while yet he encompasses the infinite). These limitations clearly must then apply to him in his creation, which had a beginning and will sometime have an end, yet are *like* the infinite. While THE CREATION PROCESS is going on, from the alpha point of God to the omega, *time* is moving forward and *change* is happening continuously. The beginning is not the same as the end. There is a great and growing *creative* difference and distance between the two. Time is moving through the infinite. In the beginning, nothing is complete, and much is lacking. Much creative work needs and must be done to bring about a completion, to arrive at an omega point.

How does this apply to us? How does it apply to good and evil? How does it apply to the Truth that we experience in this world?

Let's imagine what happened when God willed to create the world and the persons like Him/Herself. First of all, God created because **God is a creator** and cannot be otherwise, so he had to put his creation in a dimension within the infinite—Himself. **God creates what he knows.** Creation is the *experience* of the knowingness of God being willed by the Holy Spirit. We know this condition in this dimension called *time.* In *time,* creation takes place. The world and its people did not happen all at once, except in the mind or knowingness of the infinite God who **is** all at once. You and I did not happen all at once in time. It took time for us to be conceived, be born, grow, change, live, and die. All of these things and human life on our planet are in an evolving creative process with its experiences. *From the beginning,* we all are missing or lacking something, in fact, a great deal. We suffer what we call *evil* in our humanness for all that we lack, all that is missing. That which we are missing or lacking is that which God is, perfect knowledge and love. This is in no way *the fault* of the human being who is always developing or evolving toward a point of completeness, the omega person of Christ. He has shown us the way to completeness, to wholeness; but in spite of our best efforts, we all still fall short and suffer evil in this imperfect state called humanness.

Who thought it all up? Who created it all? Who has the virtue to *accept* it all? He who is TRUTH. Truth is fact.

God our creator reveals that, above all, he is virtuous and has **accepted** responsibility for what has come about as a result of creation and with his creatures. He has done this *through* Jesus the Christ. *Jesus has saved the virtue of God.* He saves us and brings us to his omega person if we have the will to follow his way.

Can Truth be explained in another way? Poor God who is all-powerful is also helpless, so vulnerable, so wise, so loving and giving, openly unshielded, victim and conqueror. God is more than Truth. God is full of wonder, beauty, compassion, *mystery* and unconditional love for his creation and his creatures.

"Why did God allow all this to happen to you?" Perhaps it is to show whoever is interested in knowing that Christianity is still evolving and all the rules and regulations of an institution have not improved upon the way of Christ but is yet to live that way. Another point of view is to say that God still loves his people, sends his blessings, gifts and love to all, often through the least likely of his little ones. He keeps leading us forward to our hearts' desire with gifts of wonder, which are just ahead . . . closer to the omega point.

Someone once asked me, "If God is good then where does evil come from?" I hope I can remember my response.

God knows both good and evil. He is *Creator,* and when He creates, He creates what He knows—not for the purpose of creating either good or evil, but this is what we as creatures experience in *creation.* Yet, God has a *way out of evil* and has given that "way" to us in the person of Jesus the Christ. We can and must evolve with that way. Nothing is perfect or complete at the *beginning* of anything, much less creation, which is always underway. The remainder of all evolution must be in the direction of the virtuous and good. Time, running through the infinite, leaves the lesser, or alpha of God behind and moves on toward the completion, or omega point of God, which is toward the perfection of all creation—the Reign of God. God has given himself, in the person of Jesus, revealing his knowledge, and his love to his people of the world. Acceptance of people and the world of creation is what Jesus has taught us. What will his people in this world now do with God?

I cannot keep letting you down, my Lord. The thoughts you give me need expression. Thank you for this energy in the work I do. Your patience is more than I deserve. You are good, kind, and generous with me, my love, and I've come to give you thanks and praise. I sing praise to your glory. You are glory revealing . . . and is there any adequate way of telling?

X

Imaging the Creator's Function

More than creator, you are the artisan of all artisans
in every way, working through every *particle* of life,
creatively moving with light in a multiplicity of elements,
generating, germinating, developing union,
reproducing every kind of life in all creation,
revealing and illustrating the image of your functions
in this cosmic laboratory as designer of life.
You are called a potter, a weaver, builder,
painter, designer, and physician. Yes,
a master craftsman, healer indeed and more;
For doctors of every science stand in awe of
the meticulous designer of flesh and bone,
Spirit, blood, brain and brawn.
The arrangement of this chemistry mystifies the mind.
Where is the place this organizing energy began?
In space and with time a recreation of the infinite
Spirit, the Crafter of evolution has given birth
to a world from the Eternal Function of union
with our *Father and Mother* who are **one** in all,
duplicating, *reproducing* their life's energy and
Orderly design in nature everywhere!
Your life produces all seed.
All seed reproduces your life.

The bugs, the bees, the plants and trees,
all animals large and small, but the greatest
image from the infinite mind is
the woman and man like the Makers of all.
God, may the grand simplicity of your unions be
seen and praised by everyone everywhere.
You are a world of revelation here in your creation,
within this hallowed womb.
Let the world be silent, listen, watch and take notice!
Something sacred happens in all relations.
God *is* in the act of Love!

2003

XI

Ways of Union

The story of Catherine of Siena reveals a very beautiful soul. I cannot help but wonder what her early spiritual education was like. Since she was only seventeen years of age when she had union with Christ and became his bride, how and when did she come to know that such an experience was possible? Was it through her awareness that she knew the presence of Christ was within, or had she been taught that such an event could occur and she sought after this union? What did it mean to her? Why did she wait so long (thirty years) before she chose to learn how to do a practical thing like reading and writing? How did she know . . . ?

I ask these questions because this idea of having union with Christ was never introduced to me during my Catholic education of eight years, at least not in any way that was discernable and personal. And union with Christ, becoming the bride of Christ as an individual, was never taught to me in any way. I had only heard that "the church" was the bride of Christ.

Reflecting upon my own experience of Christ, I did not recognize that it was he who was talking to me in my childhood and young-adult life until my awareness changed at the age of twenty-seven years. Could it be that it was part of "God's plan" that the church was not to instruct me, or the people around me, about the possibility of "mystical union" with Christ—the possibility of becoming the bride of Christ? Do ordinary Catholics know about the possibility of this experience in their lives today? I could not have named this experience when it happened to me. Why hasn't the church taught lay people about this event?

How could I, or any of God's lay people, have known about such a privileged event? The secular media knew of such events, at least in an outward way. Once I saw a movie with Audrey Hepburn in which she was to become a nun. She wore a wedding gown and was to become a "bride of Christ." This seemed to me an initiation of sorts, a strange ritual that did not seem like any sacrament that I knew about. Anyhow, I did not have a call or intention to become a nun. The *rules* I had heard about for nuns seemed to be a bit silly (1950).

Once when I was a child, a priest asked me if I wanted to become a sister. Hesitantly, I said, "no". Then he asked me what I wanted to be when I grew up. "I want to be a priest" was my reply. He looked and me with a smile and said, "It looks like the next big revelation for the church will come from outside the church." I recall that experience vividly. At that time (1949 or '50), lay people were probably considered to be *outside* the church.

There came a time after Vatican II *and long after my awareness changed*, that I knew I had experienced a spiritual encounter with God. But I could not have put a *name* to this event, and in my humanness, I thought and expected that there would be something more. Was I supposed to believe that "the kingdom of God" is a spiritual event only, for individuals only? Could human beings have spiritual union with one another? Can this spiritual union be awakened in the sexual union of two people who love one another? I will give a definite **yes** to that question. How is the earth and all that is in it and the people upon it ever to become God's kingdom? Who would tell me?

It is as though these human expressions must be used as symbols of that higher reality. Yet this must suffice if we are ever to know *about* God and the infinite Trinity that God is. I believe the writer of the Book of Genesis wrote in mythical or symbolic terms about "the beginning" of creation (which seems to be in the collective consciousness of human beings as it is told many times over in various religions).

This event about "the beginning" I see as having happened in the heavens and we human beings live out the result of who God is through what he designs in creation. (I believe that God creates what he knows.) Jesus Christ accepted the consequences of the creator's image in the world. In other words, that which human beings have come to call "original sin" occurred in human consciousness when there was an attempt to describe what happened in (paradise) the heavens. Could we consider the possibility of God our Father having *union* with his Love, our Mother? If *union* of human beings with God is possible, then it is part of the human consciousness to seek this, and I suggest it is the repetition of the Creator's image and function. What I am expressing is a sensual spirituality that, mystically, I also apply to a higher, much higher, reality. Yet everyone on earth should *know* that the Spirit of God is forever seeking union with His/Her creatures. And in the consciousness of creatures, there is that *need* to seek union with the Spirit of God. And do we not seek that love of God in one another also? Carl Sagan would refer to the Creator's union with Love in a scientific way as the *big bang*. How long shall I struggle to introduce religious people to the spirituality of the sexual and sensual, as the Creator has made us, in the Creator's *image and likeness?* God is not only our father but also our mother! They live in me. They live in all of us—the Son, their Body! Our Father is all knowing and our Mother is all loving. We are created in the union of their likeness—the Trinity, the family—individually and collectively.

While the saints and the church of not long ago disdain the things of the flesh and the world, I say, "Thank you God for everything! I see you everywhere! I love you everywhere, in every thing and every body. I shall never deny what you have given me to see and love!"

Catherine of Siena speaks of a "gentle truth." I have seen the beauty of this. It is revealed in all the love that is found in life. But I have also seen and experienced the harshness of truth, which is not to be feared but accepted as fact and overcome with courage to set us on the path to virtue. The virtue of God has been shown to us through Jesus Christ. He has accepted it all, everything that has been lacking since the "beginning" began—the harshness, the sins, the evil—and it became him—he who is "complete," all good and more.

It is up to us to imitate Christ, accept this life, this world, this flesh, our humanness, and our imperfections, which are due to our incompleteness that has come to be known as sinfulness! "Forgive us our sins as we forgive others who sin against us." God helps us to evolve into more complete persons every day of our lives by acknowledging and accepting our imperfections and overcoming them.

Let acceptance of sin against us swallow us up and kill us as it did Jesus. For all that we *accept* causes our spirit to grow, to be brave, and to be strong and gives birth to new life—the resurrection of Christ within. Nothing can harm us. God, who has taught us the way of virtue through his Son, has given that virtuous spirit to us. The way to do away with evil is to overcome it with *acceptance* and remain good. The virtuous, who by enduring violence, *take heaven by storm.*

This must also be considered. Much, if not most, of that which is in the world, our lives, our flesh, our humanness, is good and must be accepted as such. Where is God? God is everywhere. There is nowhere that he is not! He is evolving in us, and in our world. His spirit that is given to us must be used for the benefit of all creation.

I do not like to dwell on sin or evil, and I do not think much about it or of it. I do not deny that it exists or that I too am lacking much, which puts me in the category of a sinner, but to think upon God, love, and goodness is so very, very profitable. Even while we are imperfect and lacking in so much, God is still with us! All that needs to be done is think of him, be with him, love him and his creation; all else falls away. His presence is here, there, and everywhere for the asking, thinking, and praying.

Upon reflecting about what the saints have written, I have found their thoughts (de Caussade, Catherine, Teresa) very wonderful, beautiful, and good. They speak of *ways* and *paths* to reach union with him. But what is happening in their union with him? Catherine has been given instructions on "how to" get to God, and it is all well and good, but I want her, him, anyone to tell me about God! If there is a love relationship going on, tell me about that! How do lovers speak to one another? It is true that there are experiences for which there are no words, but the Song of Songs gives us an indication of what the love of God is like when experienced in the flesh by lovers who encompass each other with a spark of the divine.

I had not been instructed in any of the ways of these saints, though I recognize my experiences in what they say. So where do my directions come from and how did I get to know God except through His Son, Jesus Christ, through *His Cosmic Son—the world body.* Truly the Master Christ has taught us the way to be in union with him and with one another.

It is Jesus who has shown me the way, all the way. The teachings in his good news were all I had to know. I must give Christ all the credit. I will announce his way to the people of God again. The city streets should be walking with the saints of God who reveal the very self of Christ to us. All anyone need do is *hear the word of God*, believe and follow it!

I believe the seeds of love should be planted early in the mind of every child or childlike mind, where the innocent heart believes and receives this gift without reservation. It is from the God of love, the Holy Spirit, that spirituality grows, at any age, in any circumstance, whether awake or asleep. There is this power, this force, this energy, this action that is so overwhelming that there are no words to describe its awesomeness. The experiences of life or death cannot explain or overcome it. Love is as God is.

I cannot attempt to describe *ways* of attaining union with God. Jesus has done this better than anyone I know or could ever know. *"Believe me that I am in the Father, and the Father is in me."* *(Jn 14:11) Love* between the Father and Son *unite* them in union with one another. Love *unites* us to them.

I can reveal my many conversations with my Lord. In these, like many lovers, we reveal ourselves to one another, discover each other, teach and learn. In this relationship I am always the pupil. He is always my inspiring teacher and lover.

While there was much energy surging throughout my being while writing these previous pages, it continued throughout the day and into the night where I was restless with the thoughts that would not let go. My soul is glad to release and express the thoughts that have come to me. Let the seeds fall where they may. It is my prayer that they will reach fertile soil!

May 20, 2000
Revised October 2004

XII

Reflections on J. P. de Caussade

The title and theme of Chapter II, (Page 36), of *Abandonment to Divine Providence* is *Embrace the Present Moment as an Ever-Flowing Source of Holiness.* He states, *The activity of God is everywhere and always present, but it is visible only to the eye of faith.* These are the words and ideas of a mystic, a holy man who lived three hundred years ago, Jean-Pierre de Caussade.

He is speaking out of his time in history and out of his experience and knowledge, and out of love. There is something special and constant here that time and age do not change, and that is love.

When de Caussade speaks of *ever flowing* and *activity* of God, the word that comes to my mind is *energy,* or *spirit,* not just the source of holiness, but the *force* that creates or develops holiness to its recipient. It is seen from century to century, not just by faith and in spirit but through the sciences also.

God has increased our ways of seeing him. How we see is dependent upon the age we live in, the increasing knowledge of creation and the wisdom that is forced to develop for *its* proper use. Our experiences of life in the world inevitably lead us to the life and spirit of God.

What we see, we who live in faith, is a God who is creator, lover, and brother in all that is, who deserves worship and praise, and all that we have to give. God and his creation display signs, from alpha to omega, which say, "I Am."

To grow and gain faith to me does not mean I must kill or destroy my senses as de Caussade suggests. For to me, I am learning and gaining knowledge through my senses constantly, and de Caussade is too if he would accept it. For he states, (Page 40) *There is no peace more wonderful than the peace we enjoy when faith shows us God in all created things.* Created things are taken in through our senses. And when we use our senses to "see" God everywhere, then that which is external to the senses can become transformed into symbols of a higher reality—a spiritual reality. The elements of the world become the elements of spirit. The external is internalized, reflected upon, spiritualized . . . mystified.

I like and believe what de Caussade says: (Page 50) The *present moment always reveals the presence and the power of God* (energy). This is true if only time is taken to think about it. A person must be quiet and attentive to that moment. Sometimes we must deliberately take this time to reflect or meditate. Sometimes God takes us unaware, by surprise, and what is experienced in that moment speaks, even shouts, God is present! A transformation takes place in the soul, from heaven to earth, from earth to heaven. A prayer is experienced in union with God and with revelation of him.

In chapter II, de Caussade so often speaks of the will of God. I have to search my memory as to what this will means to me. With regard to acceptance of God's will, how shall we know, by love, law, life's experiences, or teachings? How can we always know what God's will is? Will it be after the fact of an event or surrender in helplessness? The Serenity Prayer comes to mind.

> God grant me the serenity to accept the things
> I cannot change, the courage to change the things I can,
> and the wisdom to know the difference.

When de Caussade speaks of passive loyalty to the will of God, I believe, in some way, this is what he is speaking about.

Acceptance and endurance of painful experiences is one thing, but to do this with *joy,* as de Caussade suggests, is something else. My own experience of this is with *resignation,* and then offer up what is endured and accepted. Peace settles upon a person at this acceptance and then joy enters in, usually later.

Thinking beyond that, I know it is the practice of love that is the will of God. As a child it was out of mystery about God that I practiced love of family, friends, neighbors, animals, and creation. I believe this was part of my nature. Then love came back from within, for joy was found in giving love and doing what was right. Later, I knew loving for the sake of love was a good thing to do, as it was causing an elevation to my personal being and sometimes there was evidence that the effect on another was a positive one. Love of God came easily, for he was returning and multiplying his love and precious self within me. The multiplication of love brings with it revelation. De Caussade tells this to us in the language of a mystic, and I will vouch that it is true:

(Page 69) *A pure heart and good will! The one foundation of every spiritual state.* How often I *dream* of all the good things I would like to do for those I love, all the wonderful things I would like to say to them. And often I am not free enough or able to *do,* so I just wish, want, or think about all the good I want to give or share. But often I see that those with whom I wish to share the vision of God are not ready to hear, or they will not let themselves be known and I cannot be free or intimate with such people. However, de Caussade does express spiritual freedom with elegant human words.

(Page 70), *Come, then, my beloved souls, let us run and fly to that love which calls us. Why are we awaiting? Let us set out at once, lose ourselves in the very heart of God and become intoxicated with his love. Let us snatch from his heart the key to all the treasures of heaven and then start out right away on the road to heaven. There is no need to fear that anything will be locked against us. Our key will open every door. There is no room we cannot enter. (!) We can make ourselves free of the garden the cellar and the vineyard. If we want to explore the countryside, no one will hinder us. We can come and go, enter and leave any place we want to because we have the key of David (Rev,3:7),* ("The holy one, the true who wields David's key, who opens and no one can close, who closes and no one can open.") *the key of knowledge (Luke 11:52),* ("Woe to you Pharisees! You have taken away the key of knowledge, you yourselves have not gained access, yet you have stopped those who wish to enter".), *the key of the abyss (Rev. 9:1),* (where evil is locked up) *in which are all the hidden treasures of divine wisdom (Wis.*

8:14). (I should govern peoples, and nations would be my subjects-) *It is the key which opens the doors of mystical death and its sacred darkness. By it we can enter the deepest dungeon and emerge safe and sound. It gives us entrance into that blessed spot where the light of knowledge shines and the bridegroom takes his noonday rest. (Song of Songs, 1:7). There we quickly learn how to win his kiss (Song of Songs 1:1) ascend with confidence the steps of the nuptial couch and learn there the secrets of love—divine secrets which must not be revealed and which no human tongue can describe.*

What de Caussade is describing in symbolic or in a mystical way is really the glorious freedom that love can bring—a union of discovery and revelation and a joy that only those can know when they enter into the kingdom of God, which is within each one of us to know. Such words bring lightness to my spirit and lift me to the presence of God. Then de Caussade says, (Page 70), *But what am I saying? We must praise this love, but only because we are possessed by it.* (!) Amen.

I went back to Chapter I, (Page 24), and it was nice to see that de Caussade and I were in agreement: *To be actively loyal* (to God's will) *means obeying the laws of God . . . and fulfilling all the duties imposed upon us by our way of life. Passive loyalty means that we lovingly accept all that God sends us at each moment of the day.* It is that simple. Love God with your whole mind, heart, and soul, and your neighbor as yourself.

Jean-Pierre de Caussade has seduced me into reading more about his wonderful thoughts of wisdom and experiences of God and the loving actions of all those about him. His work and his words help me to discover in a new way my own experiences of God. But I have never thought in terms of abandonment. (Page 62), he says, *The state of abandonment is a blending of faith, hope, and love in one single act which unites us to God and all his activities.* With regard to faith, Paul tells us that faith is belief in that which we cannot see. I once lived in that faith; but now I believe that my faith has become sure knowledge, as I "see" God and *know* him. Faith in him is no longer required. To know God is to love him in all ways, in all circumstances. Now I have to ask, what is my hope? My hope is in his word to me, and I shall not surrender it. Even though I can understand his word in a spiritual or mystical way, my hope and my prayer is that his word also speaks of human reality and shall become so. "Thy kingdom come, thy will be done on earth as it is in heaven."

In chapter IV, (Page 75), I think I am starting to see the active exercise of abandonment. *Those souls called by God to the state of self-abandonment are far more passive than active, yet they cannot expect to be relieved from all activity. . . . Thus we have two duties to fulfill: we must actively seek to carry God's will into effect and passively accept all that his will send us.* (But this has been part of my nature.) His words are pure wisdom, and suddenly they have very great meaning for me and a large problem that has been tormenting me has all at once been answered. Thank God for Jean-Pierre de Caussade. He still guides the direction of the spirit.

2000

Permission to quote from, "Abandonment to Divine Providence", as translated by John Beevers, has been granted by Image Books Published by Doubleday.

XIII

A Letter to Teresa of Avila

My dear sister and friend, Teresa of Avila, you are an excellent woman! If you were near me now, I would cover you with hugs and kisses, tell you that you are a holy and intelligent woman and that you shall never be considered stupid as you call yourself. Today you and your sisters would know and believe that you are equal to men, and in fact, my dear woman, you are way out in front of a vast majority of men, though in your humility you would probably disagree with me. I wish we could converse about spiritual matters. We would agree and disagree on matters of the world, God, womankind, the spirit and the flesh.

Your reasoning is so excellent that you would win any debate we might enter into. Your experience is rich and deep, and you have educated me greatly about my own experiences of the spirit. For this I say "thank you" with all my heart.

Now let us begin to examine some of our experiences together, and may the good Lord help us to understand each other.

The *Interior Castle* is so wonderful! It is like a spiritual mystery story, and I was anxious to find out what was going to be revealed in each new room of your castle!

Teresa of Avila, I have something special to tell you, and I wonder if or how many of your sisters or yourself started out with this kind of experience; I was twenty-seven years old when I found myself in the sixth or seventh room of the mansion that you speak about. The Holy Spirit was bringing a deluge of beautiful and enlightening thoughts to my mind. I was in this room of "the castle" for many years, but then I went backward. The church literally locked me out. That is one reason that I slipped backward. Like many of the priests and advisors of your day who did not recognize the spirit at work, the same is still true in these times (though I do now have a spiritual person to confide in). Not finding acceptance in or with the church, I thought, "Well, my experience of God is not important to them; perhaps they see it as a false or a wrong way of thinking. But they really don't *see* at all." And as one priest said, quoting the scripture, "John says we must test the spirit." I bravely told him, "Test the spirit!" In my heart I knew that God and I were right! Even so, later I still backslid and sinned seriously. Still I believed that God was with me and accepted the role of Hosea for me. He always calls me back and I always come back.

While God was doing a supernatural thing in my life at the age of twenty-seven years, I knew it was special, but I did not know how special until I read, *The Interior Castle*. At this time, I recognized the other rooms in the castle too. I have been in all of them at one time or another.

In the third mansion (Page 60), you said, *For if when He tells us what we must do in order to be perfect, we turn our backs upon Him and go away sorrowfully, like the young man in the Gospel, what do you expect His Majesty to do, for the reward which He is to give us must of necessity be proportionate with the love which we bear Him? And this love, daughters, must not be wrought in our imagination but must be proved by works!*"

Works done in love, Teresa, is very important, I agree. However, when there are times or conditions that will not allow this, our imagination uses *goodwill* and works within the soul.

Teresa of Avila, you are correct. I have never thought of trying to be perfect, though I do my best to do what is right and love always, in all circumstances. It is foolish, I know, but even in bad circumstances, I wanted good and expressed love for love's sake. Can what is considered to be wrong sometimes be right? I wonder. Sometimes I think yes. Sometimes I think no.

(Page 61) (I write these words reluctantly, but it is truth, for all the time He lived in the world, He did nothing but serve.) Now I cannot help but wonder if you wonder about serving *in the world,* and if you thought this might be a calling? I know things were different then from now. Women were thought to be of little importance and did not have much self-esteem, except perhaps with one another. Even to yourself, you do

not give much importance, and I do not think that humility is the reason for this; though I believe you are very humble.

On page 64 and many other pages, I read of your desire to suffer. I have a difficult time with this attitude. I myself have never had a desire to suffer, but I know that this is the first time in my life that I admit I have suffered much, but very little, practically no physical suffering. Suffering has been in my soul (spirit). But I will speak of that no further at this time. So please do not desire to suffer. There is suffering enough in the world, which comes without wishing more suffering upon yourself. It just needs to be offered up to His Majesty with acceptance and that suffering energy is transformed into spiritual growth and presence energy.

In this fourth mansion you say, *(Page 73) This spiritual sweetness arises from the actual virtuous work which we perform, and we think we have acquired it by our labors.* You are making a distinction about the natural and the divine with regard to sweetness in prayer and spiritual consolation. The key to both of these is love, my dear sister. Love is giving, and when I am doing something in nature (in my everyday world) or some spiritual practice, it is love that I am expressing and the energy of God within me that is being put to good use. And yes, that spiritual sweetness arises on both accounts. It is given to the Lord on both accounts and He always gives back more. I cannot refuse his gifts. He does not refuse mine. I am hoping we understand each other correctly (?).

I should have mentioned it before, Teresa. You are wondering if your sisters will remember what you have written but you believe it will not be lost because you say, (Page 36). *Wise and learned men know them quite well, but we women are slow and need instructions in everything.* Women are not any slower than men are, Teresa! I hope in your heart you do not believe this. In the past, even up until recent times, men have prevented women from being educated and having knowledge! However, God has educated you as he has educated me, by the Holy Spirit! And the other thing you know . . . knowledge of *self* becomes knowledge of God. S/he is our very self! What you have written has long been remembered.

(Page 77) *O Lord do Thou remember how we have to suffer on this road through lack of knowledge! The worst of it is that, as we do not realize we need to know more when we think about Thee, we cannot ask those who know; indeed we have not even any idea what there is for us to ask them. So we suffer terrible trials because we do not understand ourselves; and we worry over what is not bad at all, but good, and think it is very wrong. Hence proceed the afflictions of many people who practice prayer* . . . You have that one right, Teresa! Let me tell you about Truth.

Teresa, I want you to think about this with me, for I know you are a woman of wisdom (in the image of God) who has come from much experience of life in the Holy Spirit and is a gift of God.

When the uncreated came to be created, there was a *beginning* to what was created and is still being created. Though the uncreated is complete and perfect, the created is still in the process of becoming . . . Think about Revelations where we read, "I am the Alpha and the Omega, the beginning and the end." At the beginning, nothing is complete or perfect, but when complete or finished, it is, or should be, perfect. Building the rooms in your castle is how a person is built. Building the world, being a co-creator with God is building our cosmic Christ. Jesus is our omega person, perfect and complete, as God desires us all to *become.* It's a process, and you are very right in saying we suffer because we **need** to know. If we were as complete as the risen Christ, we would be as perfect as he, and we would have all the knowledge and understanding that would eliminate suffering. We could carry this thinking a bit further and ask God, "Why didn't you make the world complete, as in the uncreated, all at once?" But reason says, in this dimension of time, it takes time to create, it takes time to know—so we suffer in our lack of knowing. The Son of God accepted what has come about as a result of our Father and Mother creating. (This is Truth.) He suffered. We do what He did; accept what is lacking or not known, until we come to his omega state. He is the way . . . we follow.

I hear you when you speak of suspension of the faculties, but I have not done this often enough. But sometimes, *I must* do this. I am very impetuous and I thirst to know. It is hard to quiet myself because of this. When I talk to our Lord, I get right down to the matter at hand and tell Him what is on my mind and in my heart, and I am guilty of not practicing quiet times more often. But that situation will change very soon. I think I am rather primitive in prayer compared to you, Teresa. You must pray for me, please. I have some problems and I need to be close to *His Majesty* more often. He is so good and generous—always there when I turn to Him, and I must turn to Him more often! But I do turn to God in conversation, and the Holy Spirit teaches me something new all the time.

Presently, I think I recognize myself in the fourth mansion (Page 85), where I am wandering about and there are times I believe I am in the seventh mansion (where I lived so long but left). Sometimes I feel like I'm in a ball game, but in a different ballpark than all the other players because I see truth differently than most others. I'm trying to believe that I am not wrong and that the Holy Spirit has revealed truth that is fact and God who is eternally virtuous accepts himself and what he has created, which I do too. I love him no matter what. God is God and how shall we know him except through him in Christ and in us being and becoming . . . I bet you can follow my thinking, Teresa, but I don't know if you would agree. Yet knowledge is increasing. You did not hear much of anything about evolution long ago; but today, it's in our face and we see the knowledge in the world mushrooming, escalating at a speed of light. (Not quite literally) I guess you never heard such an expression anyway. Wisdom is needed in our world immediately to know how to use the knowledge that is coming into being. I love all the things you say, Teresa. With the knowledge of today, what would you tell the world? Your *Interior Castle* is still good for all time to be sure. As I read about Prayer of Recollection (Page 90) and other kinds of prayer, I say, "Yes, I've been there" and I recognize the condition. In this fourth mansion (Page 91), you give warning, *There is one earnest warning which I must give those who find themselves in this state: namely, that they exert the very greatest care to keep themselves from occasions of offending God.* This is a fair warning, Teresa. Yet, my dear woman, I think the majority of our human race does not think if they do or do not offend God. Unfortunately, I have been among the numbers who have offended God, though I have not done so with that intention in mind. It has been out of thoughtlessness—doing my own thing, for which I am sorry. Yet in my heart, I never deliberately set out to hurt my God, my self within. *"Father, forgive them, they **know not** what they do." (Lk 23:34)* He is merciful, and we need to praise and thank God for his mercy and forgiveness.

Teresa, there you are again saying women are weaker than men. Who has told you that lie? Do not believe it! And you repeated this in the fifth mansion. I know how you all seek this precious pearl in great solitude, but please do not have contempt for our world. I know you saw things differently then, but you would see God in the world these days because of the knowledge we have accumulated, gained, and have grown by—not that we are any smarter, you see—it's just that there is more to know, but it is still wisdom that the world needs.

In this quotation, the way you express union with God is more precise and accurate than I could tell. *(Page 101) God implants himself in the interior of that soul in such a way that, when it returns to itself, it cannot possibly doubt that God has been in it and it has been in God.* Amen to that, Teresa. This is true, true, true (fifth mansion). I can never have the slightest doubt that *His Majesty* and the Holy Spirit are alive and active in my life.

Yes, we are restless butterflies. Once God has taken possession of us, we want to know him more and more and there is an eagerness to look for him and find him in new ways—always. I have not nor have I ever found myself longing to suffer great trials as you suggest, Teresa, but life in the world has no shortage of trials. So we advance in the Spirit of Christ as we overcome, by acceptance, these sufferings and trials.

(Page 113) . . . daughters that the silkworm has of necessity to die; and it is this which will cost you most; for death comes more easily when one can see oneself living a new life, whereas our duty now is to continue living this present life, and yet to die of our own free will.

But you must not doubt the possibility of this true union with the will of God.

Here, my dear sister, is what happens when you are being begotten from above, as Jesus told Nicodemus. I am wondering why you do not quote the words of Jesus more often and if you have a Bible available to you. Remember what Jesus said? *"Amen, amen, I say to you, unless a grain of wheat falls to the ground and dies, it remains just a grain of wheat; but if it dies, it produces much fruits."* (Jn 12:24) We have died only to be born again into new life from above.

You are so correct in speaking of His Son to show us the way! And the great commandments—love of God and love of neighbor—this is an imperative! At every turn, God is one with us and we with him in the living of this energy we call love!

Just a word, my dear sister, corporal union (p. 118) is not a thousand leagues removed from spiritual union. (The celibate church knows little or nothing of these matters and does not teach about this fact, in truth and beauty. Lay people who know of these matters think little of what the church says but does not know!) Yet I blame you for nothing, Teresa. The heads of the church must answer to God for maintaining their ignorance on these matters. I must tell you, Teresa, I cannot separate the sensual from the spiritual, not in this life. I can see that you are trying to do this. But you know as well as I that God is everywhere. The very elements of your human body are spirit. Your elements, both physical and/or spiritual, existed when, before, after, and since God created the world. If it were not so, how could I know you now? (pp. 74-75).

Further, let me tell you about when we experience God in a sexual way. We no longer refer to it as *the grosser part of the body.* (Page 100) The body is beautiful, Teresa; God has made it so! From my experience, when God inhabits the soul, it does not matter if it is in a corporal union of two souls with him or the union of a single soul with him. He possesses love. Love possesses him!

As we travel through these mansions, Teresa lets us know that God is very much with us and he can, as he has, taken such possession of us that *we wonder if we belong to ourselves.* We begin to know we belong to each other. He awakens, enlightens, reveals, and teaches. He may stay for a glorious minute, hours, days, weeks, months, years, but he stays! The soul sings his praises, gives thanks, tells of his glory, becomes overwhelmed with his knowledge, love, and understanding—all the virtues. He is present and seen everywhere!

Teresa is gifted by God to show how his Spirit works and moves in each host which he indwells. There is no doubt that the guidance that God gave her to capture his movements in the human person has aided thousands of people over the centuries.

I have learned much from this saint of God. On page 139, I have discovered names or expressions for some of my experiences—like spiritual or intellectual locutions. And I do recall being told by a priest at the age of twenty-seven, who was quoting Jesus, "Be not afraid, it is I." That message benefited me greatly.

With regard to the messages that he has given us, I am supported by your words. On (Page 142), Sister Teresa, you say: *It may seem to the soul that everything is moving in the contrary direction to what it has been led to expect, and yet, even if many years go by, it never loses its belief that, though God may use other means incomprehensible to men, in the end what He has said will come true; as in fact it does.* Now how this comes to be no longer matters as much as the way it comes to be, and I can accept his word on either or both levels.

I have not thought much about my experiences as you have, my dear sister. There have been many, of different kinds. These blessings and gifts are more than I could ever deserve. And I do not know why God put his hand on me and chose to give me so much. I am grateful to God from the depths of my being. I would not change a moment of the pain or joy I have experienced in gaining this *oneness,* which is union with him. But I desire to give this knowledge to the world of people.

Words of yours give strength to my spirit. (Page 156), *Our Lord wants everyone to realize that such a person's soul is now his and that no one must touch it. People are welcome to attack her body, her honor, and her possessions, for any of these attacks will be to His Majesty's honor. But her soul they may not attack, for unless, with most blameworthy presumption, it tears itself away from its Spouse, He will protect it from the whole world and indeed from all hell!* How reassuring can one be! Thank you, Teresa!

On Pages 160 to 161, it is interesting the way you speak of out of the body experiences, and I wonder if you recall what St. Paul said,—*"I know a man, who fourteen years ago, whether in the body or out of the body, I don't know, only God knows, was caught up to the highest heaven, and heard words which no one can speak." (2 Cor 12:2-4)* I believe Paul was speaking about himself in the third person. I also experienced this when God in His mercy relieved me of a particular anguish I knew, which, promptly after, I completely forgot. A little later, I recalled the experience and wrote about it in this poem.

See poem: Ascent from Desperation

No, my dear Teresa, it cannot possibly be due to fancy; it is a genuine experience of the Spirit. Today, this kind of experience is recorded many times from people who have been "clinically dead," for a short time.

Now I really wish you would not have such contempt for earthly things, as you say. I don't know how ever the church came to have such an attitude for God's creation!

The world may put us to the cross, but so what? New life is the result! And after the mental persecution in contemplation within convent walls, doesn't the same thing happen there?

About knowledge and self-knowledge, you are very correct. (Page 162) *These are the jewels which the Spouse is beginning to give to His bride, and so precious are they that she will not fail to keep them with the greatest care!* Amen.

But what a strange confessor you had that he should blame you for having raptures with your Majesty. (Does anything ever change?) It's good that you listen to God and not to men—as I do myself! We are a great pair you and I, Teresa; we have a lot in common. I shall really treasure your thoughts—your book—always.

Having knowledge of our Lord would definitely make us want to celebrate—throw a party and tell everyone about Him, laud Him with love and praise, and let our joy be seen (p. 168). But when this cannot be done, when it is not permitted, it is as though we are being consumed in the fire of hell! It is a terrible thing to have the knowledge of God and have it rejected. God lets us know his pain. So perhaps the sorrow that you speak of (p. 170) is for our sins, and I might add for the sins of others who do not know of spiritual heights.

The more you speak of being with God—our Spouse—the more I know I have been failing to be present for him—like a wife who is not there for her husband. This is going to change very soon! I promise myself—my God. Not a moment of our precious love should be lost. I shall meditate 'til the cows come home or till we have our fill of each other, again and again.

Teresa, what are you saying when you say you want to keep God's favor secret? No more secrets please! When God revealed himself to me at the age of twenty-seven, I was filled with joy, delight, love, energy, and knowledge. But I was also quite suddenly very angry with the church who I believed kept God a secret! The presence of God is a marvel to me. I can never fully comprehend why this wonder of wonders has come to me. Yet I love it. Instantaneously, in need, he is present. Quicker than lightning, he makes himself known. He will not let us forget, for truly he forces us to see him everywhere. He is in charge. He may let us wander hither, thither, and yon for a spell, but he knows we always run back to him! We can cry for mercy and forgiveness, and what does he do? He loves us! He makes my heart leap with joy; he is so perfectly wonderful. Teresa, some things you speak of that may be "secret," are the things that are inexpressible. This I can understand. But we will tell all that is expressible and none shall hold us back!

This *Divine companionship* (Page 210) of which you speak is the blessing of blessings. What would we do if we could not be free, trusting, loving and intimate with him? Life would not be worth a pinch of salt! I have never been able to be free with any human being as I have been with him and he with me. Still, it would be like heaven to know that freedom with another human being, as I have known with Jesus. But that would be because I could see Jesus in him.

In this seventh mansion, you mentioned the difference between spiritual union and spiritual marriage. You pick everything right to the bone, and I love it, though perhaps I myself am more casual about detail. But I am not knowledgeable about many things in detail, so unfortunately, I generalize a lot. It is my hope, dear sister, that I understand what you are expressing also. This we must give more thought to, Teresa, (Page 113) . . . *the Betrothal has no more to do with the body than if the soul were not in the body, and were nothing but spirit. Between the Spiritual Marriage and the body there is even less connection, for this secret union takes place in the deepest center of the soul, which must be where God Himself dwells,* . . . I cannot disagree that God is in *the* deepest center of our soul (spirit, being) and at this presence, nothing else, is thought about. It may also be said that wherever our consciousness is, that is what we are present to. He is throughout the mind, body and spirit that is our being. He takes possession of us completely, wholly, even though consciousness of the body is forgotten about at that time.

Thank you, my dear friend and sister in Our Lord Jesus Christ. God has given you crystal clear thoughts for your *Interior Castle,* for the benefit of a multitude of believers. (In addition, Teresa, God has heard your prayer for the Lutherans and all the rest of them that you have been praying for too.)

June 8, 2000

Permission to quote from "The Interior Castle", translated by E. Allison Peers, is granted by Sheed & Ward, an imprint of Rowman & Littlefield Publishing, Inc.

Reproduced by kind permission of Continuum International Publishing Group.

XIV

Reflections on Matthew

There is a link built into the Gospel of Matthew from the Old Testament to the New Testament. He has done this by way of connecting the genealogy of Jesus from the days of the early patriarchs down through the line of David to Joseph and Mary, the parents of Jesus. Within this link is the activity of God who spoke through his anointed ones, the prophets, those he had enlightened who pointed the way to the coming of the Messiah. Having established the history of Israel and Jewish heritage of Jesus, Matthew then proceeds to tell the story of Jesus, beginning with his birth.

He tells a good story—real and interesting. There are plots and subplots, actions of good and evil, joy and pain, celebration and isolation, acceptance and rejection, confusion and love; it is a very human story, which had its origin in the divine. These events have happened throughout the history of humankind and continue into these end times.

The one great difference in all the events of the world was the coming of the Spirit of Christ into the person of Jesus when he was anointed from above. That difference brought heaven to earth. That difference brings salvation to humankind. In the invitation and imitation of that Spirit of Christ, the people of the world have an opportunity to change the world and by the grace of God, bring heaven (the kingdom of God) to earth once again.

The life of Jesus ushered in a new age. The old values needed to go. Laws pertaining to the external and superficial were no longer valid. Jesus was so radical, he taught love; this would be the new law encompassing all law. The anointing and enlightenment that Jesus was given was far greater than all his predecessors. His goal was to reach into the hearts and minds of people he touched. How he worked to teach his people a new way of thinking, believing and acting, but his people were not able to open their hearts and minds, for they were trained in old ways and were stiff-necked in their beliefs. *Change* was not an acceptable option, particularly for the scribes and Pharisees. The new way that Jesus had to offer was more than they could tolerate. Who could love an enemy? They were taught from old to hate an enemy. The new way was too radical for them—the man must be mad. Yet crowds were attracted to him and followed him, they had hope because of his words and ways. He revealed the mercy of God and unconditional love for them. Those who were accepting were the blessed ones.

The Sermon on the Mount illustrates the essence of Jesus' spirit, an example to follow. It was there that Jesus gave his followers a beautiful string of pearls—*the Beatitudes: (Matthew 5, 3-10,12)*

"How blest are the poor in spirit, for theirs is the kingdom of heaven.
Blessed are they who mourn, for they will be comforted.
Blessed are the meek, for they will inherit the land.
Blessed are they who hunger and thirst for righteousness, for they will be
*   satisfied.*
Blessed are the merciful, for they will be shown mercy.
Blessed are the clean of heart, for they shall see God.
Blessed are the peacemakers, for they shall be called children of God.
Blessed are they who are persecuted for the sake of righteousness, for theirs is
*   the kingdom of heaven. . . .*
Rejoice and be glad for your reward will be great in heaven. Thus they
*   persecuted the prophets who were before you."*

The religious leaders of that day did not give the people that kind of consolation, enlightenment or love. What good news "for people who lived in darkness!" There was *hope*, a gift from love. How their hearts must have swelled with joy in the belief that someone could care for them so—that God was on their side!

Recently, a peacemaker died—the king of Jordan. This man was a Muslim. The actions of this man during his lifetime became Christ-like. He worked for peace among nations and the betterment of humankind. His love for peoples was apparent. What did he know of Christ? I believe his eyes and ears became open to the spirit of love and he showed himself to be "a child of God," as did Gandhi, good Pope John XXIII, Martin Luther

King, Mother Teresa, Dorothy Day and countless hundreds of thousands who have followed a path of peace and love.

Jesus has given us a wonderful way to live through his examples and teachings. *"Do to others, whatever you would have them do to you." (Mt7:12), and he emphasizes the commandment: "You shall love your neighbor as yourself" (Mark 12:31).* It is important to love *one's self*, to the point that the very self of one is and becomes God within and with us—"Emanuel." Once we have learned how to love ourselves it will be very easy to love our neighbor. The sayings of Jesus reveal him to be the greatest spiritual leader, psychologist, and teacher who has ever lived. The wisdom of God lives within him. He has the anointing from above.

Jesus begins to make enemies as he proclaims the good news to people who hunger for and hope in his words. He is merciful, and his way of teaching his belief is liberating to those who "see." His desire was to enlighten his followers in order that they would have insights into the Spirit and life that he knew. The religious leaders are stern and falsely righteous. What good Jew would heal on the Sabbath? Their hearts are hardened. They do not comprehend the message of love, mercy, and knowledge that is God's gift for them.

As Jesus begins to reveal himself and his destiny to his disciples, it is apparent that even they do not understand. But as events begin to unfold, they would understand. At the suffering and death of Jesus, his followers lose heart and courage. They scatter for fear their own lives might be taken from them. Jesus prayed for courage and strength to fulfill the mission that his Father has entrusted to him. Then the total surrender: *"Father, into your hands I commend my spirit" (Mt 23:46).* Although the body of Jesus died, his Spirit cannot be quenched. The *seed* that germinated from that body broke open the earth and there was a resurrection to a new life with the Spirit, which Jesus promised. Now the Holy Spirit would give understanding to the apostles and disciples. Their minds would become enlightened and aware of the depths of the teachings that Jesus had given them earlier. The Spirit of Christ is alive forever, in Christian, Muslim, Jew, and Hindu—any and all who will accept the gift and way of the law of love, which brings the blessings of awareness and enlightenment, food for the souls of all God's people.

1999

XV

My Favorite Way to Worship

The words and the *promise* that Christ gave to us are real. *"If you love me you will keep my commandments. And I will ask the Father, and he will give you another Advocate to be with you always, the Spirit of truth, which the world cannot accept, because it neither sees nor knows it. But you know it, because it remains with you, and will be in you. (Jn14:15-17).* The Advocate, The Holy Spirit, who lived in Jesus has been given to his people.

The People of God in a Charismatic church is my favorite model of what the church is, and can increasingly become. In this church the Holy Spirit leads the gathering. In this service to God, all his people participate in a spiritual way and we are drawn together into the humanity of God-with-us. *"I am the vine, you are the branches. Whoever remains in me and I in him will bear much fruit, because without me you can do nothing." (John 15, 5)* We are all connected in our relationship with God and each other as we gather around the table of the Lord and sing songs of prayer and praise. The Body of Christ is where the Spirit of Christ is at work.

The Holy Spirit loves the prayer, the praise of people. When this happens, freedom and genuine spontaneity takes place. The gifts of God are given for the benefit of all his people. The Spirit of love is alive and moving with enthusiasm; that's the Spirit of God awakened in people.

Around the table of the Lord we offer our gifts, share our stories and connect with one another. There is a spiritual communion—a relationship that binds us in unity with Christ. In this body of people our spirits become attuned to the presence of God. We wait in expectation for the Spirit to move. A peaceful energy settles around the people. A word of knowledge is given and praise and prayer arise. Each heart has its communion with God and all look toward the table of plenty and the offerings that each one makes. A transformation upon the table and within each person takes place. We have participated in sharing the body and blood of Christ within this community of God's loving people. We have been fed with the elements of the earth, transformed in the Spirit of Christ. We have been nourished with the energy of God.

The human energy we spend comes from God and is offered back to him upon the table that we gather around. The People of God are always spending and offering up the energies of our endeavors, which continually gives growth to the Spirit of Christ in us and in the world of people.

When a group of God's people gather together to give praise to him and ask his blessings, special events begin to happen. The Spirit of God descends upon his body to which he has given his gifts. The presence of his Spirit becomes known, and people move and act as ONE. A reading from scripture, a word of knowledge, a song, a shared experience, speaking in tongues, an interpretation, and *unity*. Revelations of one's relationship with God and people becomes known. There is harmony in a reading, a teaching, prophesy, a prayer, a song, or petition. God is revealing himself to his people. All those in the Spirit recognize the presence of the Spirit. The Bridegroom has entered His Bride. A lovely relationship is taking place. That which is sacred becomes revealed to those in spiritual union with this presence. Peace and a time for quiet are in order. The interior life is explored and the human spirit knows it is on sacred ground. There is *new life* that sings aloud, letting God know that all that we are and all that we do, we offer to him. The Spirit-filled community share, give and grow by the light of Christ in one another and the joy of our celebration remains with us.

"As a body is one though it has many parts, and all the parts of the body, though many, are one body, so also Christ, For in one Spirit we were baptized into one body, whether Jew or Greeks, slaves or free persons, and we were all given to drink of one Spirit." One Corinthians 12, 12-13. This was the beginning of our church. This is the future of our church.

1999
Revised 2006
All Bible quotations are from the New American BIBLE.

1

Mystical Ride

I went on a mystical ride
Perhaps at the age of reason.
Someone put an apple in my hand
And told me I should smile.

Come follow me,
There are stories I must tell you.

There was a mystical voice
Which spoke inside my head.

Listen carefully, little love,
I've messages to send.
There will be those special times
I'll whisper in your mind.

I sought after you in need,
Believing with all hope,
Weeping for protection to
Keep me safe, wise and true.

If the mystical one would
Grant my wish . . . , my prayer,
I would have safe harbor.
She would guide me in survival,
Through a threatening, lonely world,
With dangers everywhere.

Follow your heart but be alert,
Heed the law of love.
Do unto others as you would
Have them do to you.

Keep the golden rule and
Protection will hover about you.
Play the games that children play,
Work hard as women do.

Learn and be alert.
Listen for my words.
Do all your seniors tell you, but,
Do not do as they do.

Be with me as time moves on.
We're in for a glorious ride.
We're bound together forever
Into a new creation,
The Promised Land—
His Kingdom Come.

2

Flight in Search of God

The *now* is here for you at last, so
Thus you come to me.
You drop your earthly wings behind
And come to me in search, to see if
You can find a little wonder in my Being.

Tell me what you see and feel.
Don't be just automation.
Observe this time discovering
Answers to yourself.

Look, then look again,
Witness what you see—
The *now*, this cosmic forever,
Which is only a part of Being me.

*Gemini Flight 1965

3

Approaching Him

With a powerful praise
      I approach
The city of my Lord.
        His ear has caught
My words of love for him
        And he is aglow with delight.
His presence comes flowing over,
        Attracting me all the more strongly
To him.
        I praise him with all my might and
He enters in . . . .
        Awakening every molecule of my being,
Filling me again with his wonderful life.
        My God, how you love praise!
And I am glad to please you in this way.
        Magnificent is my living Lord.
He is so good and
        I have often failed him-
My love in so many ways.
        Yet, whatever I do, I praise my God and
By his Spirit he touches me and bids me,
        "Come."
I dwell with him.

1960s

4

Wildflower

I've watched you grow, breaking out of the soil
Which held you in its bounds—
A wildflower, drawn up by the light of life.
From all corners of the earth the Spirit moved,
bending you to and fro, sweeping you up and down.

He saturated you in the muck and mire
as fertile food in which to root and grow out of.
Intensely the rains beat down.
Yet you stood firm, held your ground
and were not washed away.

The seeds you drop upon the earth are
strong in your strain,
increasing in every season.
You thrive in the garden of your maker.
His nature is the sap of your life.

The fruit of his flower is blooming.
A wild flower has grown and
Solomon in all his glory was never
arrayed as this one.

5

Expectations

Joy leaps up from deep within.
Soon I shall be alive with life
 at the touch of your Love.
Living in anticipation of your coming
 requires all my devoted attention.
But for your thoughts, I'd be alone
 and there is nothing better for me
 to do than think of you.
Now I cannot do, but be, yet
 upon your coming I shall no longer
 just be, but shall will to do.
You will bring new life to me
 and I shall live anew!
What are you but life to me!
 You are the cause of my yearning.
 You are the source I find fulfilling.
You are not long away;
 And my desires I will contain
 until the day it is ordained
 that we be joined as one.
Your kiss is like the sun to me,
 warming me all over.
Your strong arms that draw me close,
 shield and wrap me under your protection.
I am but a child when you surround me
 with the strength of your presence.
Disarming is the heat of your love
 which melts me down for your molding.
Great is this day and the days to come;
For I am in love with you
 and God knows,
 you are in love with me.

6

In Secret

With him
Love is a silent energy,
A quiet power, an easy charm
Given as a gift from on high
And seen by those
With inner vision to discern,
Admire and enjoy.

To linger in this
Presence is to be lavished
With the essence of life.
And I am high with happiness
When he is near.
In secret my heart sings.

7

Mother Sod, Angel Son

I was lost in not knowing . . .
And my pain was flushed by tears
As I rode and drove in anguish
Up the road to where the dead lay.
Oh, why do I come here?
I want to be dead.
Bury me.
Merciful God, where can you be?
I've come to you, but you are not here.
These are graves.
And there is nobody anywhere.
I only speak to the spirits.
Would you comfort me?
I do not know that you did when
I was a child, when you were alive.
But still I've thought that
We'd embrace if you were here and now.
I fling myself upon my mother's sod
Where weeping leaves me weak.

My son is here.
Over there where
The grass is new and high.
I press my fingers down to test
The softness of the ground.
Yes, here he was laid.
I never held him . . .
In my arms.

I walked above the dead and
Wish to lie at peace with them.
I do not know myself these days.
Angel-son, have you heard my pitiful cries?
And do you hear and know I'm alive?
Oh, forever young,
How do you know?
An angel took a mortal soul,
Just to come to be, then left again.
Do you know you've been?
And do you hear and
Know that I am
Your mother.
Would or could you help me, please?
What am I to do?
I'm tired and how I'd love to lie
At rest with you and comfort . . .
Oh and how I'd comfort you!
Dear one, my little son.
I bless and thank your being,
However briefly you were here.
Mother of God I love you.
Love them too.
The Love of the Lord is beauty.

Why did I come?
Oh yes, to speak with someone.
And have you heard that
Today there is no one to
Turn to but the dead.
But they live!
O Christ, my God,
They hear!

1968

8

I Care

Everywhere there is he
   to be drawn out by
      the magnetism of thought in me.

He will not leave.
   He is the strength I bear.
   I love him so.

His thought will never rest.
   Constant his truth keeping
     ever aware—

Glorious unsounding tongue is heard.
   Talk, talk, talk, "I care."
     There is no time

Lost in the infinite.
   He is
     to be remaining.

9

Bearing Being

O God, my God I cannot comprehend
    the vastness of your Being until the end . . .
You have said, and it is true,
    I cannot bear you without life anew.
In my being I've felt you and
    I could not contain the love,
the joy, to know you are!
    Again I'm weeping streams.

Continually you come, bringing
    light to this cell of
a dreamer in dismay,
    "Do not be anxious or afraid."
I will bear my knowing, loving,
    seeing in you fully,—this gift
from the oceans of Being.

1965

10

Liberate the Spirit

His thought will raise me out of bed
    to liberate the spirit stirring in my head.
The moon's past full when nature calls
    silently, up again, awake!
I am all here you know,
    escape, escape, escape.
Here I'm locked in a cell of flesh
    reaching beyond the beyond.
Within and out my spirit flows
    to satisfy a hungry soul and
ease a yearning body.
    To give your thought is given.
To live your thought is lived in
    and love is caught up to
The Spirit of Being the Almighty.

11

Purple Profusion

My seed is fallen but not upon the ground.
Around a metal table and upon a wooden floor,

There is no fertile soil in here.
Without the earth I cannot give birth to new life.

My seed it seems must be dusted away.
And my flower?

How long can it remain
Alive without being pot-bound?

12

Glory

Look and see the Glory of the Lord about you.
From the moment I conceived of knowing
My Lord, it was you who gave new life to me.
And there was nowhere that you were not.
In all creation your wonders were beheld by me;
And I glory in all you're becoming . . .
Even into your end perfection.
Where are there words to express these endless
Awesome marvels which I see?
O God, my love for you outshines the sun on high.
The stars of heaven that you set afire
Now play around me.
The way before me you have paved
In a path of moonbeams.
With perfect precision your spirit moves
And I am struck with awe in view of
The splendor your Being reveals.

13

Woman of Wisdom

You flow through my thoughts mother mine.
I heard and saw you in my mind.
    And there, O powerful beauty I beheld
    a vision so wonderful, of what you are
        forever, an immense elegance,
        illuminating imagining.
Oh, sweetness of life, to savor
    your pleasantness brings a rising joy.
        Your innocence germinates gentle wonder
        and a bud of bewilderment blooms.
Oh, woman of wisdom be my consolation.
    I know you well and dearly.
        I know your innermost soul.
            Ever shall I hold you
            by purity of heart.
You are triumphant woman of wonder
    with lively expressions so tender,
        ever awakening, stimulating, exhilarating
        life to lofty heights alluring.
You are a pleasure to ponder.
    Your presence humbles the heavens.
        and earth is struck with awe.
Blessed is the eternal womb
    birthing Christ from above.
Spirit of Love, woman of God, mother mine,
    you are
        ever our beloved.

1983

14

Joy of Today

Bursting with Joy
I am today—
    The bright hot light which flashes
    across the summer sky
        and clouds which creep over the mountain side.
Each drop of rain to come am I.
    My little one knows a strong caress.
    His laughter sent out is my song,
He's blest.

What are the other bits of joy
    that come my way?
    Oh, the hymn about his Pyx,
so lovely, my thought was there and
I became he who held the world
    in his fingertips!

    Oh loving Joy,
you never cease to come to be.
You just release me for a while
    to change and be found unexpectedly,
    as if you're in disguise
until the now in which I find . . .

    I will borrow your joy
    when thought overtakes me.
Wherever you are
your love will create all
    I see by you in me.

Teach me, Lord, by all I see.
Keep me Love in humility.
Purposefully I pray giving thanks for joy.
Possess me ever in your selflessness.

15

Doing His Thing

Listen all you people gathered here,
From the coastlands to the mountains
And all around the world.
Listen to the new song and
Sing it out with me.
Look at the world and see with inner vision,
The energy of creation.
Let your mind awaken and your spirit arise.
Take notice.
The Lord is doing his thing.
From above the love of Christ is pouring down.
And we who are but grass drink in his reign.
So that we may be like him forever.
Love is present and plentiful everywhere—
Seeking, searching, looking, yearning, hoping,
Giving . . . for new souls to enter in.
It's his love we sing the "new song" of.
Listen with your life!
Extend your being to openness.
Absorb his way, his truth, his life.
Be born again in his Spirit.

1968

16

To Be Himself

To be himself a man must know,
    it's love that leads the heart and soul.
Brothers, friends or other men
    will give advice to solve
Any crisis at hand;
    Never to know the depths you know.
What can I do but the same thing too?
    Let love lead a man to be himself
where he finds the heart of his soul.

17

Journey in Christ

Rejoice with me and be glad, for the Lord our God has come.
It's not just for a visit; he's here to stay. His Kingdom's come.
And *love* is the rule of his reign.
He taught me his ways from the days of my childhood.
He spoke to my mind and his words became branded upon my brain.
In troubled days he was with me and made me alert
To mistakes I made.
He lifted me like a babe from the deprivation
In which I played so helplessly.
He lifted me, wrapped me in his holy cloak, then carried me away
To his fountain where I was bathed, made clean and new.
He loved me as his child, and he became my father.
Through the years, down all life's paths, his love has never left;
Even though I wandered away, here and there, now and then . . .
When I was unaware . . .
But he is patient; gently he spoke to my heart of stone
Remolding it with his fire of love, turning it into a heart of flesh—
To beat with feeling as his own.
Tenderly he called me back.
It was the attractiveness of his words that healed my ear.
I listened. I heard! I thanked my Lord.
God, you have touched me. I can hear . . . I can see! . . .
Upon his coming he enlightened me.
"The Spirit of the Lord is upon me."
"I come to restore sight to the blind."
This light of yours is so intense,
I'm lost in the beauty of your wilderness.
It's here you've led me to let me learn the truth and love of God and man.
I praise you, Lord, for the days of my wandering are over and I am free.
"The Spirit of the Lord is upon me.

He has sent me to proclaim liberty to captives,
Release to prisoners, those in darkness, unjustly bound."
My wandering days are over,
This light has led me through the life of Christ
From birth to re-birth, from death to new life!
The Spirit of the Lord is upon me.
He has sent me to bring glad tidings . . . to heal . . . to comfort . . .
And to place a crown upon you who mourn, and
Ordain you with the oil of gladness.
Thank you, Lord, for bringing us good news.
Praise to you for your glorious revelation,
For your Being and your coming, for all your people.
Your light has shown upon us and your word has led us home.
Glory to God for spiritual favors.
Glory be for everything.

18

Need to Express

Tell me words!
Some new inspiring vital words!

Words which express
To infinite excess the

Love which burns
To free, to know,

Which returns in growth
To disperse my soul!

To give again as best one can,
Like a messenger of Being.

19

My All

Good God, my Lord, help me
    not to harm our love again.
Forgive my selfishness.
    It happened in forgetfulness.

Keep me ever watchful.
    You are too good and wonderful to hurt.
Blessings upon blessings have been mine
    because you love me so.

I cannot count the ways or times
    you've lavished your gifts upon me.
Great God, larger than life
    I love you!

You are ever present, my protector,
    guide, and lover of this spirited child.
It is you who have been everything to me,
    My true mother, father, brother, sister—my all.

You were there when I opened my eyes.
    You made my limbs and body strong
so I may run to you.
    You released me

from the prison of narrowness,
    paved a way out of the wilderness,
nursed me from the fullness of your breast,
    and fed me from the richness of your table.

Why are you so wonderful!
    Oh, because you are divine.

We must declare a celebration,
    send out all our invitations.
Nourish all in fine relations,
    We'll sing and dance with jubilation
And yield to God the glory due.

20

Thanks and Praise

Thank you Jesus for
breaking the power of Satan.
He has no hold on love.

My heart is glad, for
from my mind a song so sweet is
flowing from my tongue.
Amazing grace from Jesus Christ
has saved me for himself.

My God, you have taught me how to die
and live again in you.
And in your life my Lord of love,
destroyed forever is Satan, sin and death.

Good God, I'm glad and thankful
that you live in me.

Your strength upholds me.
My courage is from your convictions.
Your presence sustains me.

Mercy is heaped upon enemies
until they are enemies no more.

Your unbounded love amazes me,
and your might suspends me in awe.

The ways and movements of your
energies are marvels to wonder about.
How great is the Lord my God?

Guide and move in harmony with your Being.
Your word O Lord is assurance and
my confidence is upon your mighty foundation.

All you who are lost, come,
let me show you *the way.*
You, the depressed, the oppressed, the hungry,
the homeless, the chained;
you the burdened, the weary, the naked,
the sick—all of you in need!
Follow me, take my hand.
I'll lift you up; and lead you
over into the Promised Land.

Look, the day is new and
bright with warmth is the sun.
The grass is green and the day is young.
Life is new.
It's yesterday the trumpet blew.
Your freedom has begun.
It dawned with the rising sun!

My anointed one has broken
the shackles of evil.
He has touched the world with love
to heal its wounds forever.
He crushed that evil power
and broke that evil one.
He did it all with love,
my wonderful Son.

Father, the seed of your Woman has grown
to a fullness which has carried us from
the depths and darkness of hell into
the marvelous light of your eternal life.

Kind and always merciful is
my Lord to his people.
A new world of freedom has been won.

Christ paid the price in blood, with his life,
for all God's children to live in this new heaven,
beginning NOW, in this his new creation.

It's a bountiful land the Lord has led us to,-
bountiful and free, a land of milk and honey,
bread and wine and every good nourishing element!
This world—his heavenly body provides for us
his food—the energy of life.

The Lord has led us, he is our King, and
we are the flock of his keeping.

O, the might of his will and the glory of
this love that guides and sustains us.

Indeed we are a people blessed
among all peoples he has known.

Our Christ has led us home and
from his throne he reigns forever.

21

Joy of Being

Joy is with me in an outstanding way
    again today.
Because I know, by seeing through
    Feeling
The Spirit of Love which penetrates
    the senses of my being.
How can a force as great as
    Being
Exist unending without men
    seeing?
God help me in the faith
    That I have,
To move not a mountain,
    But minds in man.

22

Energy of Love

The energy of my love burns to know . . .
   My God!
You are too great for me.
   The thought of you is inexpressible
And my being longingly cries out
   For this tangible, untouchable
Infinite God so loveable!
   My God, I love!
I know!
   I love life!
I love you!
   In a body of emotion
Is your Spirit freely stolen?
   It is the Love of me
Who is to be revered.

23

Uninvolved

It wouldn't be right for gentlemen
    such as we,
After all someone might get
    the wrong idea.
We are Christian as you know
    but our caring mustn't show.
We'll be polite and nonchalant
    and let Being do his doing.
We'll play it cool and
    if all is true,
Time will come to tell . . .
    meanwhile, a body must burn,
Be it heaven or hell
    we must not show
We're Christian gentlemen
    you know.

1967

24

What Has Happened?

What has happened, Lord,
 to my brothers, your sons and friends
  whom you called away from worldliness
   into your service, in order that
    they might in meekness inherit the earth?

My question is *why* and
 when did it all go wrong?
  Who conceived the evil to be giver of
   the cross, with nail and thorns, whip and spear?
  Who rejected your risen Spirit and
   crucified your Love again and again?

Oh the cunning in that misconception of
 initiation into a priesthood of dead spirits,
  lifeless bones, shrunken heads-
   cold as stone.

Holy Spirit alive in my rising Omega Christ,
 give again new life to those dry bones
  and unfeeling heads, for
   they heard your voice and answered
    your call, but evil cheated them
     along the way in humanness gone astray,
      imposing its will and misplacing it
       for your own.

Free them all my Lord from unkind deeds
 done in your name.
  Let them see to the depths that
   Truth was crucified for
    Love to live!

And who will dare in conscience defy
  the design of Love's power for new life?
  The Spirit that is *re-born* is
  a new creation, a death-free person
  drawn up to the elevation of
  Your resurrected son.

So for them my Christ—
  all those who have battled for your life,
  even though they were led astray,
  lead them now, feed them now,
  to the fullest with your Spirit.

And may all your sons and daughters
  who will receive and answer your call,
  be *born again* in that new birth
  and deliver your child and spirit
  with life, bringing about
  a world renewed,
  our paradise.

"Before she comes to labor she gives birth;
  Before the pains come upon her,
  she safely delivers a male child."

    Isaiah 66

25

How Far to Here

Did I say you were far away?
  How far can you be?
    Look, there's heaven above us
and you sleep under these very stars with me.
  You walk in this world and
    you breathe this new life!
Though night is the darkest,
  its ne'er been so bright!
    For my heart with its wings
      has just taken flight,
to bring you here with me by this inward sight.
  Now it's feeling which moves me
    in wonder and awe,
by knowing you're with me
  when you are so far . . . .

26

Love Become Sensible

O Lord I have cried in the darkness and in the light.
    I have sought your friendship day and night.
And your Spirit within was my comfort.
    But my God, you made me into flesh and bones,
With feelings, as a human being.
    Christ, touch me, hold me, kiss me.
Be incarnate.
    Tell me again that you love me!
Speak with me—not just in my thought,
    But with the spoken word which my ear can hear.
Be sensible to me, my Lord!
    Let me feel your Spirit move
In your being flesh and human.

27

Golden Love

The sun was at her zenith
And told what she had done—
Placed her love in everyone.
Then her brother said,
"This is a Golden Love,
Meant for God alone."
There was recognition of
What she had done.

When time and life moved by
Love was held within—
But not held down.
Then an explosion of light spread
Her rays of love to all in her way.
All in everyone was
Pinned with love and
Given freely to, alas,
But in a shadow.

"Come from the *shadow*
With your Golden Love.
Shine bright as when
The world began, anew.
It is I the Lord you love
In everyone,
And I love you!"

June 22, 2004

28

Key of David

Let me be human, and treat me as a human being.
I am not Spirit alone or flesh alone.
Where do my dimensions begin and end?
And what are my limitations?
I am not above the clouds where no one can reach me
Nor am I an island in empty space,
I have crossed the vast wilderness of time
To be united with the likeness of my kind of people.
I am the City of our God—
The City he built up to be his own,
But . . . the city dwellers; Where are they?
Will one come out to meet me after my journey
To this, his holy place?
Where is the Spirit of Christ in someone to greet me?
Where are the songs of joy and happy voices?
And my children . . .
Who will invite them in and speak lovingly to them?
0h, how I would cry for joy to see them smile and
Know that their hearts are glad.

Christ, Key of David; Christ, Son of Man,
Unlock and open the door of Love—
The Golden Way through your gates of Pearl.
Humanity; is about to rise from its death
And with the Life of Christ, storm the portals of heaven.
The leaven of His Spirit has brought
A world of people to the day of resurrection.

Oh the Glory, the perfection of Love!
Who could be afraid of transformation!
My faith, my trust, my hope is in the Lord.
And there's truth in my knowing . . .
Christ's Spirit in people has built
The City of God, a ready dwelling,
For all in Christ who open the gates of Love,
Proclaiming the welcome, "Come to His Kingdom!"

1970

29

In Praise of Woman

In the beginning you told me who you were;
The Light had dawned—my mind could see . . .
My heart beat fast in joy of discovery.
The maid who had been veiled
From eternity 'til now
Is revealed by
The son of glory.
And I am in awe of
Simplicity—its beauty.
Oh, the wonder of her way!
Wisdom! The handmaid and mistress
Of the Lord brought forth
The master of the world.
The Word took flesh through your Spirit.
You placed him first.
He learned your ways so well,
And became servant himself.
He knows the source of his life,
And lifts you up to equality . . .
As service to humankind.
In a word—"Behold your mother."
Oh lovely lady, comely woman,
Tender mother—mistress to the word of man,
I glorify your holy name, and praise
Your everlasting Love.
Father-Creator, your Spirit has evolved.
Her Cosmic womb has birthed
Your Cosmic Son—
Your image and likeness are here
In your daughters and sons.

1976

30

Christ, Seed of the Spirit

It seems so long ago that
I conceived of your coming
    within my being.
Anticipating, preparing, and expecting
your presence, awakened, stimulated and
    enlivened my life.
And I danced with joy,
Awaiting your appearance.
    Months moved on and days grew long
     In loneliness, and alone I cried aloud to my Lord:
"Why delay your coming?"
    Your Spirit has swollen within me
And I am in anguish for this delivery."
Then the hour came . . . but
    None was with me as I brought you forth.
Still our father knew from afar,
Our child had come.
    My heart was glad.
It happened so quickly
I wasn't sure . . .
    What was transpiring?
Evil tried to snatch him away
While he was so helpless, so young.
    But the sun grew bright and
The earth swallowed evil up,
To save our child, our love, our son.
    I lived it all. I say what's true.
My Spirit has delivered a son.
Our Christ is here and
    Forever he comes
      To everyone.

1975

31

My Geranium

I am rooted in the love of earth.
My strong young branch shoots life up to me.
Abundantly delicate blossoms shower
    in rays of light and
    the fruit of my flower is
    heavily laden with the beauty of Thee.

32

God Is Being Alive

Being is the thoughts in one head.
Thought Being is Love and Truth and Beauty.
Love is for giving to Being.
Being fact is Truth appealing.
Accept *to be* as Being doing . . .
Existence holds Beauty of thought for seeing
Humans containing his Being.
Man is Being on earth to know—
To be man is more than human,
And man is man and woman!
Here on earth is man to see—
Being elemental in the now here *to be*,
With awareness of Being—no human eye seeing,
Is the greatness of oneness existing.
Love Being the Spirit is in all of man.
She gives of his knowing,
Men do what they can.
Love to know Beauty is Spirit aflame,
And Truth is the cross bearing the pain,
For Being, the person who is the head.
Now who but God could pronounce Being dead?

1970

33

Multiple Treasures

Look, mom!
We're the wealthiest people in town!
There's gold all over our grass and grounds,
Clear up the walk and down.
There's more to come with the passing breeze,
Which stir the trees to
Detach each lovely colorful leaf.
A path of gold before us lies.
Take note, look well,
Before this treasure dies.

34

Giving Unaccepted

It is for knowing . . . I cannot ask.
　　A bother I've been to many
　　and pretending can't cover their masks.

To see through eyes which told . . .
　　existence didn't come to be asking,
　　but is and was a cross to some.

Eye sees their telling yet;
　　unkind truth accepted then
　　and still.

No more will eye look upon
　　their hidden burden, me.
　　Seeking not to ask,

I will not a bother be,
　　and life possess the inner strife
　　of thought.

Who to be can hold?
　　To Be is not a weighty weight,
　　but being unaccepted . . .

When comes to be more *man* in men
　　this matter is resolved.

35

Seeking

How I would love to pour out these thoughts into words.
Then loneliness would flee, and
you would communicate with me.
Sincerity would say I'm not a prude.
O Understanding, how I search aware in you.

In times gone by, I knew not, yet
I turned to you.
Now "to know" is here and
still I turn from men to
run the beaten path to you again,
again and again.
Curiosity, be a welcomed friend.
Passiveness lends but numbness.
Understanding I cry send . . .

36

New Creation

Come in to my holy land.
My heart is calling to you my people.
Come rejoicing, loudly and with
lively new songs of love.

Increase your spirit with my life.
Fill my land and build
a brand new world with me.

I will grow with you,
producing fruits by our labor.
The now is here.
The infinite has sprung forth in time.

Inhabit my land and
my spirit will hover about you,
providing energy with my eternal sun.
Forever my light shines
brightly upon you.

Through you my life shall live.
Plentiful will be your days and full.
Just follow as I lead,
where I reside.

You my people are alive
in me with my risen son.

The earth is bursting with new life!
The sky is clear, the streets are clean.
God's city is aglow and
the crystal river flows freely.

In wondrous cycles, fruit ripens
On the trees of life.
"Come, feast from my land,
Love and enjoy our creation!"

1978

37

Star Gazing

You are too great, too huge, my Immensity.
I long to look again at the beauty of Thee,
    but my state is weak.
I cannot bear
    all that is dissolving me to less than meek.
I am mute.
I tremble beneath your glory.
You are too great, too great for
    such this state.
I will look again
    and love again the greatness
    which I cannot bear,
    but love to know.
Again I have known the warmth of
    your Spirit falling to cover me.

I am here and now with you.

Now you are here with me.

You have moved me Lord
    for my love to touch Thee.

38

Swelling Stream

Flow swiftly down the walk
to wash the ground as
you travel along.

Be increased with each
splashing drop which
quickly plunges on to your path
to become ripples round
and bubbles to break for air.

Flow smoothly in waves
over raised roughness.
Flow gracefully from a swelling
stream on to a peaceful sea.

39

Praise Him

Praise be to my Lord, for he set me in his world
And about me placed his Love.
His knowledge thrilled me and I burned for his knowing.
Now I ask him to receive my thanks.
His Spirit is moved and I am glad.
Through his enlightenment I see the world
And will his knowledge in it.
For Love he made the sun to shine,
Enthrones man in paradise and
Bestowed upon his Spirit are sons that shine as stars.

40

For His Love

Our Father looked upon his Love and wept for her:
 You have brought forth a world of wonder for me.
Look, they are like us in innumerable ways,
 And yet they have not seen what I give them
In you, my beloved Spirit.
 Our son is accepted as their own for
He is known to be begotten from above; but look;
 The daughter we've begotten needs recognition too.
She is so much like you.
 The plans we've made must be complete,
For truth she gives from the depths of her soul.
 Astray the path is sons of men.
They have yet to come to know . . .
 The daughter we conceive.
Plans we have for you in her are from of old.
 Our Word is given to them in man and woman!

41

Feelings

Not to express a feeling which is felt is killing.
Not to find a person being human brings great pain.
Sweet death, deliver my spirit from this cell
Of flesh in longing for the touch of humanness
To touch my soul.

Rest, just think on him again.

Upon the waters he stretches out his hand and
My spirit reaches out to flow over
To him whose strong arm caught me with his strength.
My tears mingled with the waters.

42

Welded Up Inside

An overwhelming tide is welded up inside
    and weights me down with depression.
Not a word, not a deed or thought can move
    my God, I cannot
Communicate to you
    for humans
Stand so far away.
    Over seas and mountains
In every direction
    I stand alone.
Where in God's name
    can someone be?
Please God, no more weights
    which are neither light nor sweet.
I cannot communicate to you my Lord
    because people are so far away,
And you and I are welded up inside.

43

Light Is Energy

Your light is energy to go, to move, to do.

When a day is dreary my light is suppressed
and I am without feeling.

But now your warmth caresses me
to move, to do, which grows to create . . .

Blessed light shine ever strong upon
and in my heart,

that always thought will come to grow,
creating all to be that's touched by me.

I do ever so slowly in time
what is ever and always eternally now.

I'll build your now as is
to be done, and help you, Love,

to reveal your Cosmic Son.

44

Earth and Seed

I've scattered multitudes of various seeds
    within the womb of mother earth and
She is pregnant with maturing life
    in her erotic creative body.
Seed grows from the infinite sea
    to earth in a fruitful land.
I've seeded plants, fish and fowl,
    animal and human kind.
All possess my vital life.
    everywhere there is
    fertile union in the heart of earth.
Flesh of earth, earth of flesh, spread your seed.
    Break open your land
for new life to feed us
    with all you produce—
innumerable living, growing things—*life,*
    reproduced and multiplied endless times.
Creation exalts at birth and sings aloud—
    Here I am again, repeatedly
    Indestructible seed.
Minds of earth now seeding creativity,
    Begin a splendid, new and sacred age.

45

Songs of Men

It's the songs of men and the love of life

Expressed in them that excites

My being with joyful emotions and

Lead me to sing and dance and dream

And while away some time feeling

The pleasure of being human.

The beat of life forces my spirit

To move in rhythm and time

With people.

1972

46

Searching

There is so much good to do, love to give and
Wholesome life to share.
But the world is all bound up and locked
Within itself is fear of hurt,
And there is no freedom there for them my
Friends to feel, to know the choice of being free.
They are captives of the darkness who
Look down and around but never within or to me.
Father, help me though I hurt to help my fellow man.
I'll reach out again and always in understanding.
Give him strength to take my hand.
And I will lead him into himself
And help him find you there.

It's not an easy journey to travel
Deep within and view the battered being
Of a world that's wracked by sin.
But begin at the beginning—
Just one step at a time.
Now you're walking where you feel
The hurts of life returning to your mind.

Call to him your healer,
Who hears your every thought.
His life will wipe away your tears
And lighten the way within.
His strength shall grow in power
To cast out evils known as sin.
The bruise will heal, the break will mend
And every scar will disappear.
The son of light will touch you
And his love will make you whole.

1970

47

I Heard . . .

I heard words which I thought
   to my love,
   but was not free to speak.
In this spirit gently we embraced
   and the joy which I felt was in grief.
Then to my Lord
   I cried for
   this time to pass,
   that my thought becomes real
   to my senses.

1974

48

Original Lover

When she was twelve, I did not see her needs
Or mine very clearly;
It's terrible not to know . . .
Not to know what, or how to do;
Not having learned to express a way to be,
How, or what could be passed on
From one generation to another?
So little was taught, so little learned . . .
We're inherited victims of original sin;
Not knowing, or knowing not what and how to do . . .
How could I know and what could I do?
Were there any books on parenting in 1972?
By thirteen she walked a path too broad
And I watched in disbelief,
Not knowing what or how to do for her.

It's more than thirty years since then.
She's been outrageous in wild, sad,
Funny, tragic, and too lovable ways.
Ripped me off, played all the tricks, begged,
Borrowed, lost or gave away all . . .
Her fault is a generous heart.
Cried in a wink of an eye, to disarm predator or lover.

I'm happy to say she's doing better these days.
She's still fun to be around in her more quiet,
Yet still outrageous and flamboyant ways.
I review these times in pain of hers and mine,
Knowing there is something sure,
Lasting through those frightening, frustrating, angry times;
No matter what she does or where she goes,
I'll always love her, as she is; though,
She needs "to know."
She's a gift, my first born—my daughter,
And I am her original lover.

2002

49

David

David, beloved son,
The Love of God has made you come . . .
You are loved to be in countless ways.
Goodness you see well and
To your bothers you do tell.

Your bright eyes dance
To tell sweet stories,
And your pleasant way is
A touch of God's glory.

David, beloved son,
You never cease to wonder one.
Angel mind is there, eye sees
How observing a little man can be.

So different is this precious child—
To know his being, worth
A while is thought to think upon
This gift my love has brought.

1966

50

About Him

A curious little hand reached down
    to pull the sand, while
folding furrows of water rolled
    over to fill the finger bowl
made by a baby-man.
    He sat and splashed
and coolness sucked his breath.
    He laughed.
His moist hair curled up
    in the back . . .
"Like the baby Jesus."
    I heard someone say
Beauty was about him.

1967

51

Allowing Himself

Busy was she about the house 'til

the child called in his baby way.

She picked him to her bosom

and dried his tears away.

Not far off his father watched and

for a moment was caught in tenderness,—

allowing himself to love.

52

Fence Climber

Little rounder, romp around,
    climb high,
get dust in your eye.
    Settle down and wipe away an irritation.
Once again, give it a try.
    But walk away, the fence is too high.
In fun frightened excitement
    he's caught.
Hide behind the door.
    For excitement moves
your little soul,
    to laughter, then run off again.
But quickly return,
    happily, to know
the sweet embrace of mother,
    surprised in
unexpected pleasant measures!

1970

53

Joy in Play Clothes

Cover me over old tattered clothes,
    your warmth and softness are grand.
Cover me over and carry me
    into make believe land.
There let me pretend to be
    the hundred things you can lend.
Cover me over in fashion again,
    to be held as you began.
Used and worn as these clothes may be
    in each is a pleasant memory.
Today once more they've given joy
    to mother while she watches me.

1969

54

By the Sea

Here I lie in the sun and
feel the sea which beats
upon me like a drum.

I am beat upon, pushed up,
sucked down and overcome.

Butterfly shells dance across my breast
and wear down, coming to be part of me.

No one counts how many or how long
I've been washed

sparkling clean, shining
by the light of noon or any moon.
Now I am the sand.

55

Our World, Our Universe, Ourselves

Personalize nature and let her speak to you in the laughing trees stirred by the morning breezes. Let her speak to you when it rains and her waters wash clean, refresh, feed and nourish the earth and our people. Let nature speak from the burning sun. Her heart is afire with love and like a great magnetic light draws life up from the flesh of our earth. Let nature speak to you from the stars, those heavenly bodies. Her energy is boundless.

Nature, you are an evolving power making life forever new. When I let you speak to me in imagery, you reveal my innermost being and I am healed as I reflect upon what you teach me.

Let nature speak to you in the clear blue sky and pure white clouds, the glistening snow, or the growth from the ground. She is a wonder at healing when revealing *yourself* to you. She is a wonder at speaking for God in our soul. She is a power to be loved.

2004

56

Spirit of God

This is the one who has been with me from the beginning—forever. She makes noble all that I am. She has given me life and breath. Now I unveil her presence to you. Give her honor and attention, as she deserves; this great quiet, infinite, humble spirit of love who has been silent for so long. Can one forget the breath she breathes, covering all she sustains . . . movements stirring life, growth, and change, this will that holds the infinite and the finite securely in place. She generates, participates in all that moves—atoms, molecules, elements of fire, wind, water, and flesh—in every body of the cosmos. Her light is seen from beginning to end by all who love her, friends of people, and all being that has ever been. Her humbleness took a cell of flesh, and divinity filled a human soul. A world of newness began.

A young girl, sturdy, strong, dark and deep, with the innocence and will of God—with all her heart and love too much to contain therein—drew an angel spirit from above. Like a brother he spoke in a quiet way. And while she quivered, she was brave. An angel said, "Mary, our father needs a son." "Here I am. Tell my Lord, his will be done."

Heaven was filled with joy and delight. The lord of the infinite danced through the night, while the stars of the heavens followed about . . . This spirit of mine is a wonder! She and my son are one in me. My word becomes their flesh. O Beauty you belong to me, tell all the world you're mine. *Comforter* of my children, you shall be comforted too. From your heart, from your head, from your breast and womb, your spirit flows and my delight is watching your spirit grow in our created dimension—stout heart, my lovely soul.

I hover over you and penetrate your being. Adversity has no chance in your simplicity. This is how I form you. This is why I love you. It is everlasting love that you possess that always keeps you strong; And Christ our son whom you brought forth has learned your way.

Blessed One! Be my mother too! You are always more and more to me, revealed in Christ your cosmic son, incarnate word is spoken, two in one. Oh, woman of God, your spirit surrounds us, your energy plays through creation. My child grown in goodness, grown in grace, go out to the entire world led by wisdom, embraced in love, and forever be etched in Christ's spirit.

2000

57

Thus says the Spirit

People of the world:

What would you have me claim for your sake, in Christ's name?
Before the Father I brought his life into Being.
His birth came to be, through my Spirit.
He claimed the title, "son of man."
How true his word and sure, for his Father is man of my spirit.
I am his witness—the event he is begotten through.
O son of man you are!
What you claim is true.
I know.
It is my love for your Father,
The man of my life who planted
Your seed within me, for I
Myself alone could not do so.
Or even could I come to be,
Except that you my son gave
Your life to this spirit who brought you forth!
Your Father has known me from eternity.
And in his knowing I too am conceived;
Yet only by my will.
And the love he knows by me
Wills to be completely known
In creation as it is in eternity.
Before all that you are came to be,
I am with you.
You my son brought forth my spirit—
My love for him.
From your very life,
From your very side,

From that place so close to your heart,
The life of my spirit flowed.
You died for love to be born.
And oh the triumph that your love has won!
Now in the world where I've come to be,
What may I claim before God, to his people?
My son has given me new life.
I am his witness.
He is my life!
My son who loves my spirit so
Has now become our Father.
He formed me as his spirit-bride
When I flowed the side of his temple.
Now his life is full in me.
Our Father and his spirit—love,
Conceive me in the other
Side of Christ, their child—
A woman and the daughter of man.
O holy infinite loving Spirit and true;
How many ways and how many times
And how many persons
You are in becoming the other for me!
Sweet Jesus, son of man, you are my brother.
Sweet Jesus, son of man, I brought you forth,
I am you mother.
Sweet Jesus, son of man,
You lead us to the Promised Land,
Becoming like a Father.
Sweet Jesus, son of man, we are joined
By him in Spirit and Truth.
I am your woman—Bride of the Lamb,
Child of our Father, spirit of Love and
The daughter of man.

1978